Tracy Klehn is a dynamic speaker and author of *Prayer Starters for Busy Moms: How to Pray All Day and Still Put the Laundry Away.* She has worked in the fitness industry as an award-winning aerobics instructor for more than sixteen years and facilitates small groups, Bible studies, and Moms In Touch prayer groups. Tracy and her husband, Russ, have two children and make their home in Valencia, California.

If you would like to schedule Tracy to speak at your next event or if you would like to download the study guide for *Growing Friendships,* go to *www.tracyklehn.com.*

growing friendships

tracy klehn

Minneapolis, Minnesota

Published by Bethany House Publishers
11400 Hampshire Avenue South
Bloomington, Minnesota 55438

Bethany House Publishers is a division of
Baker Pubishing Group, Grand Rapids, Michigan.

Printed in the United States of America

ISBN-13:   978-0-7642-0434-0
ISNB-10:   0-7642-0434-3

In keeping with biblical principles of creation stewardship, Baker Publishing Group advocates the responsible use of our natural resources. As a member of the Green Press Initiative, our company uses recycled paper when possible. The text paper of this book is comprised of 30% post-consumer waste.

green press INITIATIVE

Library of Congress Cataloging-in-Publication Data

Klehn, Tracy.
    Growing friendships : connecting more deeply with those who matter most / Tracy Klehn.
        p. cm.
    Summary: "Practical ways and encouragement for mothers of young children to make friends and nurture ongoing friendships. It includes, among other topics, the value of friends, making new friends after a move, maintaining longtime friendships, and restoration of broken relationships"—Provided by publisher.
    Includes bibliographical references.
    ISBN–13: 978-0-7642-0434-0 (pbk. : alk. paper)
    ISBN–10: 0-7642-0434-3 (pbk. : alk. paper) 1. Mothers—Religious life. 2. Friendship—Religious aspects—Christianity. I. Title.

BV4529.18.K63   2007
241'.6762082—dc22   2007028743

dedication

To all the "daisies in my chain":

Your love, encouragement, support, laughter, tears, guidance, and prayers have crowned my life with more joy than you can imagine. Please know that whether we see one another regularly or we catch only glimpses of one another through fond reminiscings, I treasure our friendship as a *gift of grace* straight from the hands of our heavenly Father.

To the daisies of my youth: Corry, Eryn, Kim A., Kim E., and Patricia

To Krista, Beth, Tiffany, and The Temecula Connection

To the original Monday "Ya-Ya's": Sue, Andrea, Liz, and Gwen

To the woman who helped me through childbirth and beyond—Nancy S.

To the best neighbor EVER, Michele

To Heather, Persa, Kathy, Jennifer, Becky, Gabbi, Julie R., Patti, and Betsy

To Shirley & Torelli: "Write on, paisans!"

To the Football Moms, *The Path* Gals, the 2nd Generation Millerton Gals

"The Greats," the Moms In Touch Prayer Warriors, and the Women of NorthPark Community Church (past, present, and future)

To Julie Luepke, Nancy, and Jodi: You showed us what "coming alongside" truly looks like

To "Good News" (Luke 2:10): Your friendship has been a healing and enlightening blessing in my life

And finally to my little Gracie Girl. Mommy prays that throughout your lifetime you will grab hold of the lifeline that Jesus extends to you in the form of an intimate relationship with himself and "growing friendships" with other sisters in Christ.

contents

Two Are Better Than One

Arm in arm we walk this road
Laughing much—God's truth we know
Together we stay strong and tight
In Christ we find our true delight

How sad it is should one fall down
All alone with none around
Why did they forfeit this gift from God?
A Chain of Friends, with whom to walk

Link arms, stand tall, look straight ahead
He lays the path on which to tread
And should you stumble in the night
Your friend will help set you aright

Two are better than one, because they have a good return for their work: If one falls down, his friend can help him up. But pity the man who falls and has no one to help him up! A cord of three strands is not [easily] broken.

(Ecclesiastes 4:9–10, 12)

introduction

A Life FULL With Girls

No one has ever seen God; but if we love one another, God lives in us and his love is made complete in us.

(1 John 4:12)

With the exasperation that only an eight-year-old boy can muster, my son announced, "Mom, my life is FULL with girls! There are forty-two of them; I counted!" We'd just pulled into our driveway, and as he opened the door and hopped out of the car he threw his hands up in the air and cried, "I didn't count the girls across the street, Mom—that makes forty-four!"

Unlike my son, when I say, "My life is FULL with girls!" I say it with enthusiasm as well as gratitude because it has been through friendships with women that the Lord has revealed himself to me in tangible ways.

When I reflect on my life, I can honestly say that it was through the bond of friendship that I was first able to "taste and see that the Lord is good" (Psalm 34:8). Over the years I have been blessed with some very special friends: There was Krista, who took me under her wing when I went through the culture shock of moving as a junior in high school—from Canada to California. Trends are quite different in these countries, and I soon found out that my short hair and pumps were out and that I needed to get some acrylic nails and big hair ASAP! And there was Beth, whom I met during my college years. Beth had the mind-boggling knack of making me laugh uproariously over the littlest things, and she ultimately led me to "eternal bliss" (otherwise known as marriage) by introducing me to my husband.

But it was at the time of my first pregnancy that God invited me into a circle of friends that I like to call my "daisy chain," and He used these special relationships to teach me about His character, His love, and His undeniable presence in my life. In other words, it was through friendship that my image of God began to heal. It was through friendship that God showed me that He is neither far off nor ambivalent toward me. Yes, friendship has not only been a gift to me, it has truly been a lifeline.

Perhaps you were drawn to this book because you love your circle of friends and you want to continue to nurture those relationships. Maybe you picked up this book in the hope that you could find your place in a circle of friends. Or you were given this book as a gift even though you feel nervous when you think about the possibility of letting other people get to know you. It could be that the idea of God working through people is a new concept for you. Maybe you've been praying for God to make himself real to you, but you didn't expect Him to do so through a circle of friends.

Whatever the case, my goal is to help women like you—women who are short on time and low on energy—find and develop their circle of friends, because I truly believe this is God's lifeline for women. I will do this by sharing heartfelt stories, creative ideas, scriptural prayers, and inspiring quotes. Using the analogy of making a daisy chain crown (yes, the kind you used to make and wear when you were a little girl!), I will walk you through the specific stages of friendship—but don't let this dictate the order in which you read the book. I give you permission to open up this book randomly, to go to a chapter that sounds appealing to you, or to find the chapter that addresses a certain issue on which you could use some input. Consider studying the book with a group of friends. You can download the study guide for *Growing Friendships* at *www.tracyklehn.com*.

At the end of each chapter you will find the following sections:

Ponder

This is the place you will find a handful of thought-provoking questions to ponder. It is an opportunity to get to know yourself better and to make yourself known (should you choose to go through this book with a group). I encourage you to grab one of those journals you haven't opened yet (I know you have a few stacked on your bedside table or on a shelf somewhere), and get your thoughts down on paper. Journaling my thoughts and prayers has had an amazing and positive impact on my life, and I believe the same thing can happen for you.

> **Thoughts disentangle themselves as they pass through your fingertips.**[1]

Getting Unstuck

As you journey through *Growing Friendships*, you might become aware that you are feeling stuck or that the chapter you just read is the place on the road to growing friendships that you struggle with.

One of the places I have found encouragement when I feel stuck, anxious, or afraid is in the book of Joshua. In the first chapter we find the people of God on the border of the Promised Land. Moses has just died and God has called Joshua to lead the people into the land "flowing with milk and honey" (Joshua 5:6). God encourages and exhorts Joshua (and us) with these words: "Be strong and courageous.

Do not be terrified; do not be discouraged, for the Lord your God will be with you wherever you go" (Joshua 1:9).

Take a moment and circle the words *you* and *your* in Joshua 1:9. Notice that God could have simply said, "God will be there," but He didn't. He said, "The Lord *your* God will be with *you* wherever *you* go" (emphasis mine).

You too have a personal God who is with you every step of the way, a God who has a Promised Land to bring you into—the Promised Land of friendship. When you are frightened, or feeling stuck, try not to beat yourself up. Turn to your personal, loving, and ever-present God and confess your fear to Him. Tell Him you believe that He is with you and that He will give you the strength and courage you need to move out in spite of your fear. If you are having a hard time believing that He is with you, confess that as well and ask God to help you with your unbelief. Belief is not something you muster up in your own strength, it is a gift from God—and one that He wants to give you. (See Mark 9:14–27.)

Take your sticking point to Jesus in prayer and ask Him to continue to deliver you from it so that you can drop the relational shackles that bind you and connect with the beautiful friends He has placed in your life. From now on when you start feeling stuck, think of it as a little yellow sticky note marking a page. Simply allow it to be the flag that it is—a gentle reminder that this is the area that is difficult for you when it comes to relationships (connecting, forgiving, speaking the truth in love, confronting, letting go). This is the area where you need healing, love, courage, or boldness. As you continue to pray and move out in the strength, grace, and power you receive, I believe one day you will look back and see that the Lord has removed those sticky notes from the pages of your life.

Pray

Over a decade ago prayer entered my life, and I haven't been the same since. One of the most extraordinary things I discovered through prayer is that God loves me so much that He is concerned about every aspect of my life, including my friendships, and that He is available to guide my every step. I get so excited when I start talking about the power of prayer! It's no surprise then, that prayer was the topic of my first book (*Prayer Starters for Busy Moms: How to Pray All Day and Still Put the Laundry Away*) and that prayer is an INTEGRAL part of this book.

At the end of each chapter, you will discover a "Prayer Starter." A prayer starter is a practical way that you can begin to pray given the subject you've just read about. These starters are just that—a diving board of sorts, which means that if you have more prayers to pray, journal, or say, then by all means continue. Do not let the amount of space in this section limit you. Get out that journal and enjoy diving into a powerful and precious prayer relationship with your heavenly Father.

Apply

This section will give you ideas to help you apply the principles of the chapter. It is full of fun, practical, and helpful hints about friendship. It is likely that there will be some ideas that are completely *not* you. I officially give you permission to shelve those ideas (or better yet, tell them to a friend whose personality fits the idea). It is also likely that you have already done or are doing a variation of these ideas, and that is great! Nothing like a little affirmation to keep you on track! My hope is that there are a few ideas or reminders that will be helpful to you or that they will get your creative juices flowing to help strengthen the bonds between you and your friends.

Lessons From "The Greats"

Whenever you see the words "Lessons From 'The Greats,'" know that it is thoughtful advice or a practical idea from a great circle of friends. I met a few of these women over coffee, and I had a feeling I might be able to glean some insight from them regarding growing friendships. They didn't let me down. Here is the story of how they earned their nickname:

"We can't all be a 'Great,'" Marion, a lovely (and lively) seventy-year-old woman said quietly. She explained that she still sometimes catches herself looking back over her life and wondering, *Where is my gift? What have I done?* When she does this she reminds herself that she has raised children who are well-adjusted, contributing members of society, and that is a great accomplishment. As I listened to this humble woman reminisce, I realized why God had inspired me to talk with her and her girlfriends. She is a "Great," and so are her friends, for anyone who can love well and inspire others to do the same belongs in the category of "Greatness."

Marion is a part of a circle of friends who have been tight for well over thirty years. Initially bonding with one another because they were neighbors with young children, these women (and their families) have taken friendship to a whole new level, and in so doing have communicated to their children, grandchildren, and the world what is possible when you *choose* to live a connected life.

Letters From a Friend

Scattered throughout the book are "Letters From a Friend." These were not all written by me or to me. They are, however, authentic letters filled with words that have penetrated souls and knit hearts together. My hope in including them is to show you that deep, honest, Christ-centered, connected friendships are not only a possibility, they are happening in your midst. I also hope to inspire you to "put feet" to your own thoughts and prayers and write your own Letters to Friends. In so doing, you will be giving a gift that lasts, and one that could make your "daisy chain" even stronger.

I am not a psychoanalyst or a therapist of any kind. I am a *girlfriend,* and I write from the perspective of one who was made aware, by the grace of God, that friendship is a gift to be given and a gift to be received. Friendship is an offering of oneself for eternal glory and an experiential opportunity for God himself to reveal His presence to His people this side of heaven.

The prayer of my heart is that *Growing Friendships* will help you get connected and stay connected so that you too can "taste and see that the Lord is good." As your hand brushes through the pages of this book, I hope that the curtain will be brushed back from your eyes to reveal the lovely view of abundant living Christ has waiting for you. Come out and play . . . your friends are waiting!

chapter 1

The Daisy Chain

"A garland or chain made of linked daisies."[1]

**Friend: One attached to another
by affection or esteem**[2]

**To the Ancients, Friendship seemed the
happiest and most fully human of all loves; the
crown of life and the school of virtue.**[3]

—C. S. Lewis

Flowers can brighten up a room and put a smile on your face. They can also be expensive if you are the one purchasing them. For most people, flowers are an "extra" and not a "must have." That is to say that if you're low on cash, or you're a starving student, buying yourself a bouquet of flowers might be a little farther down on your list of priorities than say, Krispy Kreme donuts (the real "must have").

So if flowers are not necessarily needed for *survival*, what is their purpose? They make life more beautiful with their vibrant colors and heady aromas. Perhaps they even remind us of a certain person or a certain place, or they represent an expression of love, sympathy, or encouragement.

In *The Four Loves*, C. S. Lewis writes: "Friendship is unnecessary, like philosophy, like art, like the universe itself (for God did not need to create). It has no survival value; rather it is one of those things which give value to survival."[4]

I used to have a hard time enjoying the flowers my husband would bring me. Not because I didn't think they were lovely, and not because I didn't appreciate his thoughtfulness. I had a hard time because I felt it was too extravagant to spend money on something that was just going to last a few days and then die. So my husband started planting flowers for me outside, flowers that we could keep, grow, and enjoy. Unfortunately, these plants have *all* died a slow death.

It is somewhat ironic, then, since flowers are not my forte and I am by no means a gardener, that the symbolism I would choose to use in this book is that of a specific flower—the daisy. While there may not be anything growing in my front yard, there are some gorgeous blossoms in my life. The flowers that I love to look at any time of the day or night, the flowers that I love to grow with, nurture, and enjoy, are the daisies that I call my girlfriends.

Daisies sure are cheerful little flowers, aren't they? They seem to show up everywhere . . . on hillsides, by streams, in gardens. The generic name for the daisy is actually *bellis,* which is derived from the Latin for beautiful. Daisies are indeed beautiful, and they are easily recognizable. Likewise, most people have seen or heard of a daisy chain, which is a handful of these cheerful flowers strung together in a row.

When I think of friendships, I think of these daisy chains. I think of friendships as gathering the individual flowers that are in our midst and connecting them to make something even lovelier.

When it comes to friendship, I *do not* believe that we scatter a few magic beans (like Jack, for his beanstalk) and grow ourselves a circle of friends. We are not the ones who grow friends. *God* is the Master Gardener. Isaiah 60:21 says, "They are the shoot *I* have planted, the work of *my* hands, for the display of *my* splendor" (emphasis mine).

So then, what is our responsibility with regard to friendship? *I believe that we have the choice to connect with the beauty that God places in our lives.* We have the choice to *receive* the gift of friendship and to *invite others* to do the same by extending our hearts to them. God invites us into His garden and allows us the opportunity to adorn our lives with a crown of friends.

Friendship is the crown we wear that communicates to God and to the world that we are receiving the love that He has provided for us.

**You shall also be a crown of glory
in the hand of the Lord.**

(Isaiah 62:3 NKJV)

In doing a little research on daisy chains, I stumbled onto a sweet article entitled "How to Make a Daisy Chain."[5] As I read it, I realized that making a crown of daisies is very much like developing a crown of friendships. The author describes this process in verb form—"to daisy chain." I love this because I believe the process of developing and deepening friendships is an action. We are "growing friendships"; they don't just happen to us. We are active participants.

We may have bouquets of flowers in different rooms in our homes. We may have gardens full of flowers in our yards, whether the front, side, or backyard. We may even have pots of flowers leading up our walkway or decorating the front porch. Each of these blossoms can make our lives more lovely, inviting, and enjoyable, like the roles of many of the friends and acquaintances in our lives. However, what we will focus on in this book are the flowers that adorn and decorate your *very person* . . . the close circle of friends that crown you with love, compassion, and joy; the circle of friends that holds on tightly through life's ups and downs.

Proverbs 18:24 says, "A [woman] of many companions may come to ruin, but there is a friend who sticks closer than a [sister]."

Are you ready to dive into the garden? Are you ready to open yourself up to the deep and abiding gift of enjoying and nurturing a handful (or more appropriately, a crown-full) of friendships?

Let's go outside and play. . . .

Lessons From "The Greats"

**My old friends are like my favorite pair of jeans . . . you
know, the ones that are the most comfortable
and make you feel great!**

 **Ponder**

How has your life been made more beautiful through friendships?

Are you currently a part of a circle of friends or are you more aware of the bouquets and gardens of acquaintances?

As you look back over the course of your life, when did you feel the most "connected"? When did you feel the loneliest? What were the circumstances surrounding each of these times?

What is your heart's desire when it comes to friendships?

Did you find yourself "stuck" anywhere in this chapter? Did you find a place that needs the healing touch of God or the strength and courage to move forward?

 Pray

They will be called oaks of righteousness, a planting of the Lord for the display of his splendor.

(Isaiah 61:3)

Father God, I thank you that you tell me that I am "a planting of the Lord for the display of his splendor." I thank you that one of the ways I display your splendor is by loving and being loved by friends. Help me as I begin this journey to learn and understand on a deep level what friendship is so that I can give and receive this gift.

 **Apply**

Treat yourself to a little bouquet of flowers (AND a donut!). Place it somewhere that you can be reminded throughout the day that you are "a planting of the Lord."

Deliver a bouquet of flowers (or even a single flower) to a dear friend with a note that reads, "You make my life more beautiful!"

Letters From a Friend

Dear Friend,

You are living proof that God lives and shows himself through our relationships! Thank you!!

Thank you for making my 30th special. Thank you for all the presents and time and love you continually give me. I will never forget that you came by on my 30th even though I was sick and you baked my favorite dessert.

Your friendship, support, and unconditional love bring tears to my eyes. I am so blessed to be a part of your family and so blessed that I have a best friend who loves my children and loves my husband and inspires us all. I am blessed by your marriage and the way you love each other and our Savior.

Thank you for being on the journey with me.

I love you,
Andrea

Chapter 2

Going Out to Play

*The first step in making a daisy chain is to go
outside . . . that's where the flowers are!*

**Friends invest time in one another's lives. They make
the conscious choice to "Go out and play." They see
friendship as an invitation from God to
receive what He has for them.**

I stand at the door and knock. **If anyone hears my voice
and opens the door, I will come in and
eat with him, and he with me.**

(Revelation 3:20, emphasis added)

Remember when you were a little girl and you would knock on your neighbor's door and ask, "Can Mary come out and play?" As a child you made the choice to go and knock on the door, allowing your girlfriend to decide whether or not she would come out to play. Not much has changed over the years. This is still the first step when it comes to growing friendships. It is making the choice to "go out and play" or, in other words, to choose to value friendship and to invest the time and energy it takes to connect.

There was a time in my life when I made the choice *not* to go out and play. My best friend was Nancy Drew, and most weekends I could be found holed up in my attic bedroom clutching those yellow-bound books. I feel sad thinking about that little girl (that I was). She didn't know what she was missing. She didn't know that she could have more laughter, joy, and company in her life. She didn't realize how lonely she was, nor did she realize that wounds of rejection had entered her heart and caused her to tuck herself away with a "safe" friend.

That safe friendship found between the pages of books continued on through junior high; my library card was paper thin from overuse, my battery stash running low from many late nights spent reading under the covers with a flashlight.

It wasn't until after my husband and I were married and had purchased our first home that I began to realize the potential that was available to me through friendships. At that point, I began to make the weekly choice to go out and play, and this continued for a long time.

For seven years five of us gals met together on Monday evenings at a local restaurant, occasionally mixing it up a when a good "chick flick" came to town. As I reminisce about the faces around the table those first few Monday nights, I see two friends with very young children, two friends that were newly pregnant, and one friend that was on the career track. We all had busy lives, yet we made the choice to meet, and in doing so learned the value of intentionally setting aside the time to invest in our friendships.

We spent those Mondays talking and listening to one another, laughing LOUD and crying hard, celebrating pregnancies and births, promotions, anniversaries, birthdays, and the life that happens in between. We prayed for each other through marriage challenges, work challenges, and hormone challenges, and we tried our best not to judge one another when we needed to "vent" about our children challenges.

Not every Monday was a party . . . there were some really hard Mondays in the mix. There were times when we needed to share feelings that weren't "pretty" and discuss topics that we were in disagreement over. There were times we "missed" connecting well and had to ask for forgiveness, and there were times when we lost our temper and felt like giving up on friendship entirely. Still, by the grace of God, we chose to continue to "go out and play."

As a circle of friends, we made a huge investment of time in our relationships, and the dividends were enormous. I can honestly say that Monday night lifeline helped me in more ways than I am even now aware of. My girlfriends showed me what grace, forgiveness, and loyalty were all about, and they helped me enjoy the season of life that I was in.

Were there times in those years when we had other things we could have done on a Monday night, such as chores, work, or catch up on sleep? Of course! But friendship is a choice, and there are many reasons why it is a choice worth making.

Why Making the Friendship Investment Is a Wise Choice

You've Got Help

Choosing to invest time and energy in friendships offers you the potential of having help in times of need as well as your being a help to someone else. For example, the time I tried to teach my son to go down for his nap without first being driven around the block in a car!

My friend Gwen was a year ahead of me in the baby department and so she was the lucky gal who got my call one winter afternoon. All I remember clearly is that I was "done" with the whole napping thing and that this was the day Spencer *would* learn how to get himself to sleep. The problem was that after five minutes of listening to my child shriek, I couldn't tell if I should pick him up or let him cry. In desperation, I referenced the book that guaranteed that if I followed the program rigorously, "my little sunshine" would be on a regular "sleeping schedule" in no time. The book described different types of cries, and in my inability to be a "wailing translator," I called Gwen. In a loud whisper I summed up the situation. "Gwen, I can't tell if I should pick Spencer up or not. I can't tell which cry it is. Can you help me?" She gave me a hesitant "Okay..." probably because she wasn't clear about exactly what kind of help I was asking for. I then recall *crawling* on my hands and knees into Spencer's bedroom (so he wouldn't see me through the crib slats), holding the cordless phone up in the air so that Gwen could get a clear sense of the cry I was attempting to interpret, then tucking the phone under my chin and crawling out of the room. Once I was safely in the family room, I said, "So, Gwen . . . what do you think?" Stifling a giggle, she said, "Well, he *does* sound mad . . ."

I am laughing as I write this, and when I remind Gwen of my request for help from her on that day, we usually end up doubled over a piece of furniture somewhere. But at the time I was desperate for help, and my point is that when you choose to invest in relationships, you will have people you can call when you need advice, help, or just someone to tell you you're being ridiculous (which, by the way, Gwen did not do—God bless her!). You can also be that person in the life of another.

> **If one falls down, his friend can help him up. But pity the man who falls and has no one to help him up!**
>
> (Ecclesiastes 4:10)

You Are Following a Spiritual Model

If there is a single theme that I have internalized from attending church regularly it is that God's dream for us is to be in relationship with himself *and* with people. Recently my pastor put it this way: "God is a small group." It was my pastor's way of communicating that God is connected and lives in a state of constant relationship because He is a Trinitarian God. The Trinity is made up of the Father, the Son, and the Holy Spirit, and these three are always together. We are created in the image of this Trinitarian God and therefore created with an innate need for relationship. My pastor went on to say, "To follow this model of a relational God, we must work hard to connect with people."[1]

Not only are we created in the image of this relational God, if we look to God's Word we see that it is filled with actions toward "one another."

- Show mercy and compassion to one another. (Zechariah 7:9)

27

- Love one another. (John 13:34)
- Be devoted to one another. (Romans 12:10)
- Live in harmony with one another. (Romans 12:16)
- Accept one another. (Romans 15:7)
- Serve one another. (Galatians 5:13)
- Be kind and compassionate to one another. (Ephesians 4:32)
- Admonish one another. (Colossians 3:16)
- Love one another deeply. (1 Peter 1:22)

It is only as we relate to people that we are able to accomplish what God calls us to do for one another.

"It's Just Me and God"

I have met people over the years who say that their walk with God is their number one priority. And when I look at their lives I can't help but notice that it's literally just them and God. Now, there are seasons in life when God calls us to walk even more closely with Him. He may call us out of the crowd and into His embrace by leading us to spend extended periods of silence and solitude with Him. I'll talk more about seasons just like this in chapter 10. But people who live the spiritual Lone Ranger life concern me. I wonder what they do, for example, with 1 John 4:19–21: "We love because he first loved us. If anyone says, 'I love God,' yet hates his brother, he is a liar. For anyone who does not love his brother, whom he has seen, cannot love God, whom he has not seen. And he has given us this command: Whoever loves God must also love his brother."

God loves people, and making the choice to invest your time and energy into friendships is indeed a spiritual model.

> Through friendships I have learned about God's unconditional love and acceptance . . . it's so great when I call my friends and hear their happy tone when they know it's me, or they see my name on the Caller ID, and then pick up with a "Hellooooo!!! I was just thinking of you!" I

think that's how God is when we pray . . . He sees us on
his "Caller ID." The difference is He already
knows we will pray (or call) before we do.

—Nancy H.

It's Good for Your Health and Well-Being

In Dr. Brenda Hunter's book *In the Company of Friends,* she writes,
"Women are twice as likely to get depressed as men. A major cause?
Social isolation. If we have only superficial conversations at work
or if we're home alone with small children, we are likely to become
depressed. To find our way out, we must begin to build a supportive
network of other women."[2]

You Will Have More to Give

When you invest in your friendships, I believe that you will have
more to give in the other roles and key relationships in your life.

A lot of women falsely believe they are being selfish if they do
anything for themselves, including scheduling time to go to coffee
with a friend. Constantly aware of the demands on their time and
energy from other areas (work, kids, spouse), they just keep giving
and giving until they hit rock bottom and lose it one morning. (If
they're anything like me, it is likely to occur when they get the kids
into the car for school.) The truth is that in order to have something
to give out, women need to have something coming in.

God's Word says, "We love because He first loved us" (1 John 4:19).
Out of the overflow of the love coming in from God, we are able to
love others. We cannot create something out of nothing. We cannot
"muster up" energy, love, and enthusiasm for life.

Are you feeling empty? Is there love, laughter, and prayer coming into your life? Does your cup "run over" or is it bone dry?
Making the time for meaningful friendships is one of the ways that
you can allow God to pour into your cup and into your life. Being
available for your friends is a way God can use you to refresh the

cup of another. When your cup is full (or at least not "bone dry"), you are much more able to serve your husband, your children, and your employer.

My kids were babies when I became aware of this need to monitor how full my cup was. At that time my husband would go on the occasional business trip. If the trip was longer than one night I learned (through the encouragement of some wise friends) to schedule a baby-sitter for an hour or two on one of those days. This not only gave me something to look forward to while Russ was gone, it also made me less resentful of my kids at five in the afternoon (what's up with kids at that hour of the day?) and of Russ when he walked in the door after being away.

Investing in friendships also relieves undue pressure that you might be inadvertently placing on your husband to meet every single one of your needs and on your children to "make Mommy happy." Your kids aren't meant to be your best friends. They need to know that you have grown-ups in your life who are helping you, loving you, and encouraging you. This frees them up to be kids.

These days when I am feeling "low," my husband often says to me, "Why don't you call one of your girlfriends?" or he offers to watch the kids so I can get out for a little while. He has learned that I am much more pleasant to be around and much more able to serve out of a "full cup."

> **So it is not only for my benefit, but also for the benefit of my family that I ensure time is set aside for me to be with other women. As a mom and a wife, I often find myself sacrificing to ensure my husband and children are getting their needs met without a thought for my own needs. This often ends in disaster because as the saying goes, "If Mama ain't happy, ain't nobody happy."**
>
> —Nancy S.

You Will Leave a Legacy

By choosing to be a friend and have friends, you are choosing to be an example to the little ones (and big ones) in your life. We have all heard the old adage "Actions speak louder than words." If you are living a life that is connected, you are modeling to children that it is a possibility and a necessity in their own life. You are modeling a life that is not lonely.

Just the other day I picked the kids up from school and told them we were going to go celebrate because Focus on the Family just bought over a thousand copies of my first book, *Prayer Starters for Busy Moms*. Grace (age 9) asked, "Did you call Dad to tell him?" "Yup," I said. Spencer (age 11) asked, "Did you call Shirley?" "Yup," I responded. "What about Gabbi and Auntie Andrea?" Grace asked; "and Torelli," Spencer added. By that point I was smiling from ear to ear and said, "Hey, you guys know exactly who I called!" To this, Grace gave the classic response "We know who your 'peeps' are Mom!!!"

Do your kids know who your "peeps" are?

Facing Your Fears and Taking the Risk

In friendship, there have been times when I have felt rejected, resentful, and resistant.

I was the pesky kid sister that would follow my big sister around when her friends came over. I had a single desire, and that was to participate in the fun that was being had inside Nancy's "cool" room. *I* wanted to sprawl out on her white shag carpet and read *Seventeen* magazine. *I* wanted to talk about makeup, boys, and whatever else you talked about when you entered those mysterious teen years. I wanted IN. However, no matter how much I begged, inevitably Nancy's door would slam with a bang and I would hear those fateful words from the mouth of my sister:

GET YOUR OWN FRIENDS!

Slinking back to my room and throwing myself on my bed, I would feel sad, rejected, and angry (probably one of the motivating factors for turning to the other Nancy in my life: Nancy Drew).

It wasn't until I started writing this book that I realized I have my sister to thank for one of the greatest blessings in my life . . . my friends. Her exhortation propelled me to make my own friends.

My girlfriends are a gift, and the time I spend with them, the letters I receive from them, the laughter and tears I share with them, cause my heart to spill over with gratitude. Had I been invited into my sister's circle, I don't know that I would have ever looked elsewhere for my own friends.

You too may have experienced feeling like the outsider in relationships, the little girl left crying in the hallway while the party is happening on the other side of the door. Those feelings are painful and real, but they are also in the past. I believe God has something new He wants to do in your life, and He is calling you to step out of your comfort zone and look around you. I believe He wants to bless you with a circle of friends. Your own friends.

It is no light thing to choose to "go out to play." There is risk involved, and there is the possibility of feeling pain and rejection. But there is also the possibility of feeling "known" and of having someone to walk the road of life with you. Author of the groundbreaking book *The Friendships of Women*, Dee Brestin says, "I've found that women who don't take risks don't have friends. Sometimes we don't really pray about our friendships; we just gravitate toward the person who's similar to us. Seek the Lord with a sense of expectancy about the people he'll bring across your path—even if it's women whose age or circumstances are different than yours. Then take a risk based on the Holy Spirit's leading."[3]

As I began the journey of writing this book, my fourth-grade daughter, Grace, came home with one of her own completed writing assignments—about friends! Isn't it exciting to see that the topic of friendship is such a priority to our Lord that He has an entire household "on the same page" at the same time?!

Why Everyone Needs Friends
by Grace Klehn

"This is why everyone needs friends. There are many reasons for having friends. First, friends keep you company. Friends keep you company by playing with you. Next, friends give you joy. Friends give you joy when you are sad. Last but not least, friends help you when you're in need. Friends can help you by praying. In conclusion, everyone should have friends and always meet new friends. Everyone should have friends because of company, joy, and help."

 **Ponder**

Who are "The Greats" in your life—a person or a group (past or present) that was a great model of friendship?

Did your parents or significant adults in your life have close relationships? What did this communicate to you about friendship?

If you haven't chosen to invest in friendships, is there a reason why? Are you afraid of something specific?

Over the years I have heard women complain that they just don't have any close friends. One of the things I ask them is, "When was the last time you initiated with a phone call or attended a 'connecting event' like a seminar, a retreat, or a home party?" When they stop to think about it, most of these women say they were too busy with kids, housework, or their careers to keep up with these things.

I encourage you to take a few minutes right now and think through this. Do you value friendship? Do you value it enough to take the time to make the investment to phone a girlfriend just to "catch up"? Have you gone out for lunch or for coffee with a friend recently?

Did you find yourself stuck anywhere in this chapter? Did you find a place that needs the healing touch of God or the strength and courage to move forward?

Pray

Lord, thank you for calling me out to play. I want to value people and relationships like you do and to see the time that I spend with people from your perspective. Please help me in this area. I believe there are women whom you have hand selected for me to have as friends and I look forward to that. I confess that I _____ (tell God any areas of fear, guilt, or shame that have come up from this chapter), *and I ask you for the courage to move out. Please prepare my heart to be a godly friend.*

Apply

"Going Out to Play" With the Daisies in Your Chain

Give one of your friends a call "just to chat."

Say yes the next time a friend or potential friend initiates something with you. If there are details such as baby-sitting that need to be worked out, pray about it and ask God to help you.

Talk to some of your friends about getting a girls' night out in place on a weekly or monthly basis.

If you don't have one already, get yourself a journal to record your thoughts, feelings, and prayers about friendship, and on the first page write out your top three reasons why you are going to choose to invest in friendships.

Write a commitment to the Lord and to yourself that you will invest in people.

Sample:

Lord, I choose to open the door and receive your gift. From this day forward I commit to investing a minimum of _____ a week into friendships by participating in _____, by talking to _____, and by being open and prayerful about the friends that will initiate something with me.

Letters From a Friend

Dear Friend,

You are a blessing from God, who never stops giving. It's not just the tangible ways, but more important, the intangible ways . . . Just talking to you helps lighten burdens that weigh me down. This is a special God-given gift you have, and I've been blessed by it. Whether you realize it or not, you've shown me how to live from a full cup of God's blessings, how to refill my cup when it is low, how to give back to others, and how to have fun too. I hope God has and will use me to help fill your cup too. You are an incredible woman and friend and I love that you are in my life.

Your sister in Christ,
Kathy

Chapter 3

Gathering the Bouquet

Start looking for daisies in gardens, on hillsides, by streams . . . when you find real, healthy flowers, gently pull them from the ground close to the root so you have a lot of stem to work with!

> He alone puts eternity in our hearts and gives us
> traveling companions for the journey there.[1]
>
> —Brenda Hunter

Once you have made the decision to "go out to play," it is time to start "gathering the bouquet."

Looking Around

Where are the gardens in your life? By which stream or on what hillside has God placed a potential friend? The Lord has specific "daisies" set aside for your crown. It is now time for you to look around and discover them.

> I think it's best to share an interest (birds of a feather),
> so that you can have something in common. Join a
> hobby group, like a local supper club or a book club or a
> Bible study. Or ask current friends to throw a barbecue
> and invite new people. Go outside of your comfort zone.
>
> —Nancy H.

Checking in the Front Yard

Perhaps some of the people in your neighborhood are a future part of your daisy chain.

When I came home from the hospital with my daughter Grace, I got my first knock on the door from Michele. From that day on, it seemed that Michele often found a little reason she needed to pop by for a visit. On one of those visits she commented on the fact that there always seemed to be cars in and out of my driveway. Smiling, I explained that I had a close circle of friends who knew I'd been worried about adjusting to becoming a mother of two. I explained to Michele that my girlfriends had been coming over a lot to keep me company while I recovered from my C-section, breastfed the baby, and tried to spend some special time with my firstborn, who was adjusting to the newest member of the family.

Michele seemed intrigued by this and asked how I knew these girls; I explained that we all went to church together. A few weeks later, Michele heard that our church was having a women's retreat and asked if she could join in. The rest is history. Michele and I became fast friends, our houses became interchangeable, our children grew up together, and many nights you could find us outside sitting in lawn chairs in the driveway, reading our mail next to one another while the kids rode their bikes around the cul de sac and our husbands whacked golf balls into plastic cups on the front lawn. It was a friendship born out of sheer proximity and, of course, the hand of the Master Gardener.

Who is in your proximity? Have you met the people in your neighborhood? Maybe it's time to go knock on some doors!

Checking in the Backyard

The friends that God has for you might just be in the most unexpected locations—even in your own backyard! Just because you're related doesn't mean you can't be friends as well!

For many years I prayed for a mentor. I asked God for a mature woman who would take a personal and active interest in helping me be the best possible mother to my children, wife to my husband, and servant of the Lord. After a few years of sensing that my prayers were bouncing off the ceiling, God opened my eyes to the fact that I already had a special daisy in my very midst.

After forty-five years, my mother-in-law is still married to the love of her life. She's raised three children who are all well adjusted, somewhat normal (I mean, who's completely normal, right?) Christ followers. She's been attending the same church for over thirty years, she is passionate about finding a cure for Alzheimer's, and spends time volunteering with the John Douglas French Foundation for Alzheimer's Research. And best of all, she is in love with my kids and is highly invested in being an active part of their lives.

Here was a woman who was already in my life, but I had overlooked her because she didn't come into my life in the way that I expected. My mother-in-law and I are friends, and these days we even get to minister together. I share my love of Christ to groups with my words and she with her songs.

Are there any daisies in unexpected locations in your life?

My only advice for friendship is never overlook someone because they are different—especially the chance to have an older friend. Some of my most treasured friends are my "intergenerational" friends. Conversation is easy. There's no competition, and they offer much wisdom and experience. They love with a pure love, and I have learned so much from each of these precious women.

—Sheri Torelli, author and speaker

Taking a Walk Down Memory Lane

Is there a friend that you would enjoy reconnecting with, a person that you have a history of laughing with, hanging out with, and living life with? Friends from school (high school, college), old jobs, a cousin?

After a recent move, my friend Lindsey recounts:

God works in amazing ways. He has brought old college friends back into my life that are now some of my closest friends here. One friend especially has become my dear friend in the past few months. We share a love for the Lord and have started a Bible study together. She is my "go-to" girl when I am down. Kristi is a constant reminder that God is faithful and loving.

Taking the Initiative

Author/speaker Georgia Shaffer knows that family is a big thing for singles. As one single woman recently told her, "I just want a family. That's all I want." When Georgia speaks to singles groups she teaches: "We singles need to redefine 'family.' By family I'm not necessarily referring to biological family. It could be a church family or a family of friends. A healthy Christian single understands the importance of creating a community—a supportive social network in which they are themselves, not wearing masks." Georgia goes on to say, "My family includes married friends, divorced friends, widowed friends, and friends who have never been married. And they will continue to be my friends whether I'm dating or married. As singles we need to make the choice to *intentionally* build a supportive social network and address any obstacles that are hindering that."

Whether you are single, married, divorced, or widowed, you can be intentional in your pursuit of living a connected life by taking the initiative and starting an activity, attending an event, or using your gifts and passions to serve. Some examples of this include:

- Church (especially a small group, a singles ministry/fellowship, a Bible study, a ministry team)
- Sports (taking up a game of tennis, golf, volleyball, soccer)
- Clubs (ski, garden, book)
- Taking a class at a local community college or through your Parks and Recreation department (for a degree, or special interest such as photography, sewing, dance, pottery)
- MOPS: Mothers of Preschoolers exists to help moms through relationships established in the context of local groups that provide a caring atmosphere for today's mother of young children. (*www.mops.org*)
- Moms In Touch International is two or more moms who meet for one hour each week to pray for their children, their schools, their teachers, and administrators. (*www.momsintouch.org*)

- Stonecroft Ministries is a Christian organization that provides a variety of programs and resources designed to connect women to God, each other, and their communities. (*www.stonecroft.gospelcom.net*)
- Playgroups
- Bible Study Fellowship (*www.bsfinternational.org*)
- The gym or fitness center (I know from personal experience teaching aerobics for sixteen years that the "regulars" at the gym do bond—especially the early-morning regulars; they're like a little family!)
- Charities (what cause are you passionate about?)
- Ministries

As you take the initiative to develop friendships, you might have some false starts or some closed doors. This happened for my husband and me within the first few months of our marriage.

After a few months of church hopping, we finally thought we had found one that would work for both of us—a breathtaking, century-old Episcopalian church in Marin County. Once we decided this was the place we were looking for, we jumped in with both feet. We signed up to help at the church's upcoming fund-raiser, a Holiday Home Tour.

It was while I stood as a hostess in the kitchen of one of these grand homes that I realized this might not be the best place for us to get connected. Every few minutes a cluster of people from the congregation would tour the kitchen, pat me on the hand and say in endearing tones and sweet voices, "How nice of you to volunteer to help! Now then dear, who are your parents?" Apparently Russ was having the same experience as a host in the family room. By the time we drove home that night, we knew we were still on the lookout for a place where we could be fed both spiritually and relationally.

While you are taking the initiative to make new friends, pray that the Lord would guard your heart from discouragement, and that He would help you keep your hope and sense of humor alive.

I have made friends from church, and that is one of the best ways to make friends when you are older. When you are young, it is much easier to make new friends. There are the school functions, the kids, young couples on the block—many easy ways to make friends. When the kids are grown, it is much harder to make friends.

—Jean

As a career woman with no children I have realized that I need to be very *intentional* about making new friends. Many of my friends that are mothers don't realize that they have many "natural" ways of meeting new friends because of the circles they are exposed to through their children (school, sports, extracurricular activities). I think it's a little harder for those of us without kids. So I intentionally go to Bible studies and other connecting events, and I pray that the Lord would open my eyes to the women with whom I would connect well. When He answers this prayer, or when I see a woman that looks like a potential "gal" pal, I take that (sometimes awkward) first step and strike up a conversation.

—Marita Littauer, coauthor of *Wired That Way*

My friend Marita (quoted above) is a classic extrovert and loves to be around people. Yet even she acknowledges that starting those first conversations can feel awkward at times. I can only imagine how much more awkward for those who consider themselves shy. Some of my shy friends have told me they can feel absolutely immobilized by feelings of anxiety ("What if I say the wrong thing?") and insecurity ("What if I make a fool of myself?") in situations with new people. One of the best ways to conquer this destructive cycle of self-obsession and isolation is to remember that you don't need to say the perfect thing, but simply reach out to new people with genuine interest. Here are a smattering of questions that you can ask to help get to know others:

- I love your _____ (compliment them on their hairstyle, outfit, piece of jewelry)—where did you find it?

- Do you have any plans for the upcoming (holiday weekend, summer vacation)?
- So what do you do?
- Do you work outside the home?
- How did you get into your career?
- What do you enjoy about your job?
- Have you lived in the area a long time?
- What are some of your favorite places to eat, shop, hang out?
- How did you and your husband meet?

People often feel warm toward those who are genuinely interested in getting to know them ("She's such a great listener!"). If you concentrate on expressing kindness and interest toward other people instead of being fixated on what other people are thinking of you, those first conversations will be easier to start and friendships can have a chance to blossom.

Letting the Kids Lead the Way

Depending on the stage of motherhood you are in, you have the potential to have many "gardens" to gaze into for daisies. Look around when you are out with your children. You will know in advance (if there are kids in tow) that you have at least one thing in common!

Early Motherhood
Parks
Playlands
Gymboree or gymnastics
Mommy and Me exercise classes
Lamaze class
Preschool

School-Aged Children
PTA
Sports/activities
Community pool
Sunday school
Music/choir

Preteen and Teen Years
Youth group
Booster clubs for sports
Sports/activities
School functions

Being Open to Initiation

Being open to initiation does not mean joining a sorority and going through the hazing portion of the semester; it means prayerfully responding to the women who are reaching out to you.

Is there a woman in your life saying, "We should go out for coffee sometime" or who is inviting you to her Pampered Chef (or other) home party or women's retreat? Is there a group of friends that regularly wave you over, inviting you to sit down and join them for lunch or ask you if you want to join them for a movie later? Perhaps there is a gal at the office who has offered to pick up lunch for you, or a friend at school who's asked if you'd like to study together.

Carol (one of "The Greats") told me that when her son was very young, she found out there was a family on the next street over with a child about the same age as hers. Thinking it would be nice to get the kids together to play as well as to chat with another mother, Carol walked around the corner with her son, knocked on the door, and introduced herself. More than thirty years later Carol still remembers what this woman said to her: "I have plenty of friends, thank you," and with that she shut the door. What a shame! Little did she know that in her rebuff of Carol's *initiation*, she may have lost the opportunity for one of the best friendships she could have ever known.

I encourage you to be prayerful about the women that God brings into your life. Even if you have a life full of friends, you never know why God might be leading someone to initiate a friendship with you!

Lessons From "The Greats"

Be Open to New Friends

If you want to be a part of our group, you can be . . . you'll just have some catching up to do!

Staying on the Lookout at Work

You already have something in common with women in your workplace. Why not ask someone to lunch, to join you on a walk during a break, or to have a cup of coffee? Take a look around you at work; there might be some daisies in your midst.

In reality, a few years difference in the dates of our birth, a few more miles between certain houses, the choice of one university instead of another, posting to different regiments, the accident of a topic being raised at a first meeting—any of these chances might have kept us apart. But, for a Christian, there are, strictly speaking, no chances. A secret master of ceremonies has been at work.[2]

—C. S. Lewis

Seeing Your Special Need as a Special Opportunity to Connect

Henri Nouwen says that we are all "wounded healers," inferring that we all have the most potential to heal others in the areas in which we ourselves have needed and experienced healing. This spiritual principle is captured in 2 Corinthians 1:3–4: "Praise be to the God and Father of our Lord Jesus Christ, the Father of compassion and the God of all comfort, who comforts us in all our troubles, *so that* we can comfort those in any trouble with the comfort we ourselves have received from God" (emphasis mine).

Do you have a special need in your life? A unique circumstance, an illness, a disability, a loss? With the help of the Internet, future relationships could be just a click away. There are plenty of opportunities to find out if there are others who are walking down the road you're on. Some examples of this include but are not limited to:

Recovery Groups (*www.christianrecovery.com*)

Grief Support Groups (*www.compassionatefriends.org*)

Safe Haven, "A place for healing from the trauma of abortion" (*www.postabortionpain.com*)

Joni and Friends

For nearly a quarter of a century, Joni and Friends has been dedicated to extending the love and message of Christ to people who are affected by disability, whether it is the disabled person, a family member, or friend. Our objective is to meet the physical, emotional, and spiritual needs of this group of people in practical ways. (*www.joniandfriends.org*)

Pulling the Stem as Close to the Root as Possible

A friendship that has the potential to grow is one in which both people risk revealing their whole selves to each other, not just the "pretty parts." It's difficult to make a daisy chain with a hard plastic flower, and it's difficult to be in a growing friendship when you or your friend aren't being "real." Likewise, if you only pop off the blossom part of the flower, you won't have any stem to thread through and make the daisies into a chain.

I didn't know there was something more to friendship. I didn't know there was something more to me. I didn't know that I had a stem, a part of me that I wasn't showing to anybody. I didn't know until it was drawn out by a friend who asked me deep, thoughtful questions and then quietly and attentively waited for "me" to show up.

I was the girl who had a ton of friends in high school, the girl who had a smile and a wave for everybody, the "nice" girl, the "she's-so-sweet" girl, the girl who was very concerned that everybody like her. I don't know that I consciously chose to behave this way, it just felt normal.

I grew up as the middle child in a big family and took on the role of the hardworking kid you'd never have to worry about (believing this would get me the love and attention that would satisfy my soul and lead to true happiness). By the time I got to high school I had this role perfected. What I didn't realize was that what I had also perfected was "being liked by many but known by few."[3]

This began to change when God brought a special friend into my life. Sue's listening heart drew me out and her own quiet authenticity set the tone for our friendship. "She did not talk to people as if they were strange hard shells she had to crack open to get inside. She talked as if she were already in the shell. In their very shell."[4] Sue was "real" with her faults and foibles, and this model of authenticity along with her listening heart helped me get to know myself and helped me realize there was more to me and more to friendship.

Sue was also a student of God's Word. One verse that she introduced me to was James 5:16: "Confess your sins to each other and pray for each other so that you may be healed." This verse was life-changing for me.

There is a healing that begins when you risk sharing a part of yourself, even a thought or a behavior from your past (the abortion, the affair, the eating disorder or addiction, the sexual abuse that was done to you) that you feel is ugly, shameful, and dark; and then you look around and see that there are *still* people sitting next to you. That there is a friend that is *still* holding your hand or crying along with you or nodding her head gently as she holds your story in her eyes.

This is a taste of grace. This is a taste of acceptance. This is a taste of love. It occurs most often when you risk sharing yourself with safe people. When you get that taste from the circle that surrounds you, you catch a glimpse of the extraordinary love that Jesus has for you, and you float home.

I encourage you to be real within your chain of friends, to risk being bold enough to see and share your whole self—the blossom and the stem. I encourage you to be gentle listeners with the flowers in your life so they too can risk emerging from the shadows and stepping into wholeness.

A Word About "Safe People"

In the book *Safe People,* authors Henry Cloud and John Townsend say, "Safe people are individuals who draw us closer to being the people God intended us to be. Though not perfect, they are 'good enough' in their own character that the net effect of their presence in our lives is positive. They are accepting, honest, and present, and they help us bear good fruit in our lives."[5]

If you are a person that often finds yourself in friendships and relationships that are less than healthy and possibly even destructive, if you feel like you attract individuals that are not "safe," or if you just want to go a little deeper on the topic of friendships/relationships, then I highly recommend picking up a copy of the book *Safe People* and/or a copy of Cloud and Townsend's *Boundaries*. Their expertise has had a profound impact on many lives—mine included.

Should you become aware that you are in need of more help than a book can provide, I recommend seeking wise counsel. One of my most meaningful friendships was made as I sought professional help with some patterns of behavior I had in relationships that I *knew* were not productive. It says in Proverbs 20:5, "The purposes of a man's heart are deep waters, but a man of understanding draws them out."

There are many types of counseling and many types of counselors. If you are moving in this direction, your decision about a counselor needs to be, first of all, bathed in prayer—that the Lord would guide you to the right individual for you and clearly affirm that decision. If possible, find a counselor who comes highly recommended. (Do you see fruit in the life of someone you know who is in counseling? Ask them if they could recommend a counselor to you.)

One excellent resource for counselors is New Life Ministries. (You can call 1-800-NEW-LIFE to find a counselor.)

Oftentimes insurance covers part of these sessions, but I don't recommend strictly going with who is on your list of providers. Trust the *True Provider* and believe that if He is *guiding* you in this direction you can move out in faith and believe He will *provide* the means to support it. Make an investment in your life and the lives of those around you by seeking wise counsel.

A Single Flower Does Not a Chain Make

While picking the flower at the stem rather than at the blossom allows room for your daisy chain to be made properly, collecting several daisies rather than just one creates a bouquet that you can make a chain from in the first place. Remember, the goal is to have enough flowers for a chain, not just a bud vase.

Author/speaker Dolley Carlson advises that we need to free our friends to have other friends.[6] We must not grasp so tightly to one person that we choke the life out of her.

One of the blessings of having more than one friend and being a friend to more than one person is that it relieves the pressure of feeling like you (or your friend) must meet a person's every need (more about this in chapter 8).

It's so awesome to know that when I need to talk (vent, cry, or laugh) I have a few friends I can call. Likewise, when one of my friends is in crisis and I am not available, I am relieved to know that she will not be left all by herself if I am out of town or otherwise unable to help.

One of the other blessings in having a handful of friends is that we get to see sides of one another that we might not otherwise see. C. S. Lewis reminds us that "In each of my friends there is something that only some other friend can fully bring out. By myself I am not large enough to call the whole man into activity."[7]

My girlfriend Michele is one of funniest people I know, and laughing with her is one of my favorite things to do. (Our husbands say they can hear us laughing from down the street.) But even she admits that she needs other people to play off of. She is quick and witty, but she needs material!!

Listen to what Elizabeth says about having one friend versus having a handful of friends:

> Almost two years ago, my very best friend in the whole world moved across the country. We had been inseparable. I had never had a friend like her. She was the only person I had ever met that I literally never got sick of being around. We cracked each other up, we were prayer warriors together, we finished each other's sentences. So when she moved I felt like a piece of my heart was ripped out. It was so tempting to be angry with God for showing me what true friendship was about only to tear it away from me. I still have days when I'm just lonely and wishing desperately that she was right up the street. But last night God showed me once again that she was just the tip of the friendship iceberg He had for me. He needed to take her away so I could open my heart to some of the most amazing women I could ever know. They were there the whole time, but I needed my blinders taken off so I could see.

 ## Ponder

Looking at the list of gardens in this chapter, in which garden of your life do you see the most potential for friends?

Are you open to initiation, or do you connect more with the neighbor who said, "I have plenty of friends"?

Are you real and authentic in your friendships? Why or why not?

If you needed to "chat" or were in a crisis, what friend would you seek out? If she wasn't available, what other friends could you call on?

Have you ever felt jealous or anxious when your friend(s) spends time with other girlfriends besides you? Why do you think that is?

Did you find yourself stuck anywhere in this chapter? Did you find a place that needs the healing touch of God or the strength and courage to move forward?

 ## Pray

Father God, I thank you for the many gardens in my life and I ask you to open my eyes and my heart to see the women that you want me to "connect" with. Please help me be "real," Lord; I feel _____ (fill in the blank) when I think about sharing my whole self with people. Give me courage and give me discernment. Help me know whom to share myself with and alert me to the proper timing for these conversations. Help me to be gracious and loving when my friend(s) risk opening themselves up to me. I thank you that you love me just as I am and not as I should be, and because of this fact I can risk being myself.

Apply

Host a "Neighborhood Soup Supper." Make a few pots of soup (or chili) and encourage the neighborhood to come over for a casual open-house-style event. It will give you an opportunity to meet some potential friends and to serve others through hospitality.

Give an old friend (from your trip down memory lane) a call or e-mail and spend some time just catching up.

Check out one of the Web sites listed earlier and see if there are some gathering opportunities that sound appealing to you.

Letters From a Friend

Dear Friend,

I remember the first time we ever talked. It was at Christ Lutheran when the girls were just three. You had a cast on your foot and we somehow began a conversation. I knew right then that you were a special person and one I wanted to get to know better. I never would have imagined at that time that we'd be where we are today. Your friendship is a treasure to me, and your love and support of me and my family means more than words can say. I look forward to the many meaningful and wonderful times ahead not just for you and me, but for our families as well.

I love you,
Julie

Chapter 4

Connecting the Flowers

Split each stem of the daisies by making a small slit with your fingernail and then thread a stem through the hole.

The most important thing in life is to learn how to give out love, and also to let it come in.[1]

—Morrie Schwartz

I noticed the man when I opened the door leading from the parking garage into the street. He held out a cardboard sign asking for help, and he smiled at all the passersby. The following week when I walked out the same door, he stood in the same spot. That day the man stayed on my mind even after I returned to my car and drove away.

A week later I packed a few granola bars into my glove box. After I parked, I walked over to the man and with my hand extended said, "How about some breakfast?" The man waved at me and replied, "Oh, no thanks, I'm on a diet." I was so surprised by his response that I stopped in my tracks. Seeing me there, rooted to the spot, he repeated, "No, really, thanks anyway, but I'm on a calorie-restricted diet." I turned slowly and put the bars in my coat pocket, and as I walked a question began to form in my mind:

How often have I done that?

How often have I prayed ("Lord, comfort me . . . help me . . . be with me") and then waved my hand and said "No thanks" when God answered my prayers? "No thanks" when the answer to my prayer didn't come in the package that I thought it would or should come in? How often have I refused God's blessings because I was expecting something else?

More often than not God has chosen to answer my prayers by sending me His people:

A friend to walk a lonely road with me so that I could feel *God's presence*.

A friend to bring a meal to my family when they knew I was too exhausted to cook and in so doing helped me experience *God's provision*.

A friend to speak an encouraging word to me when I was feeling down in the dumps and thereby helped me experience *God's guidance*.

A friend to aid me in a task I was dreading and in doing so allowed me to experience *God's help*.

In one of my talks I teach women the power and blessing of being an encourager in the lives of people around them. Women love this idea and proceed to take avid notes, nod their heads, and get excited about the idea of giving encouragement—right up until the point when I ask them how well they do at receiving encouragement. That usually stops them in their tracks. I know this because I am one of them.

Why is it so hard to receive from the outstretched hand of a friend? Is it pride? Is it shame (because I feel so needy)? Is it denial? Is it my fear of counting on people and being disappointed by them?

Somehow I learned that I should never be a burden. That one of the worst things I could do was to wear out my welcome. I falsely believed that my needs overwhelmed people, that my job was to be fun and entertaining, and that people would only accept the pretty parts of me, the parts that were easy to get along with and didn't need anything.

Is there a time you can look back on that made you feel your needs might overwhelm and drive people away? Is this a sticking point for you? Is it a wound that needs healing?

In authentic friendships it is important not only to give but to receive, not only to be there for your friends, but to ask your friends to be there for you and to receive from them even when you didn't ask, to believe that you are not a burden but a blessing, to risk all for the sake of a *mutually connected* friendship. In this way you are being "knit together" (Colossians 2:2 KJV).

Just as one daisy stem is gently inserted into another to form a chain, so do friends give and receive from the heart, and in so doing grow a beautiful and strong chain that can be formed into a crown.

The Ways We Connect (Areas in Which We Can Give *and* Receive)

With Spoken Words

There was a definite process by which one made people into friends and it involved talking to them and listening to them for hours at a time.[2]

—Rebecca West

Saying what's on your heart and receiving what's on another's heart (active listening), whether in person, on the phone, or in a letter, is a powerful way to take each other in and to allow your hearts to be woven together.

Kathy and Jennifer and I have been walking together twice a week for four years. We talk, we cry, we laugh, we share our lives together, and we almost always end by doing a group hug/prayer. Over the course of many walks Kathy has candidly shared her desire to be able to feel more. Aware that long ago a part of her heart was wounded, she learned to keep plugging along in life without feeling much of anything. A few years ago Kathy's infant son died. Kathy refused to let this tragedy pass her by without allowing Matthew to penetrate her heart. She has been courageously and actively walking through the treacherous and sometimes frightening territory of grief. As the three of us walking girls were parting ways just a few days ago, Kathy stopped us and said, "I have to tell you both something . . . thanks for being my friends. Thanks for hanging in there with me. I love you both and I just wanted you to know that." Her words penetrated our hearts and I could feel our chain become tighter and stronger through that exchange of words.

Kind words may be short, but their echoes are endless.[3]

—Mother Teresa

In Writing

**An anxious heart weighs a man down,
but a kind word cheers him up.**

(Proverbs 12:25)

Soon after Kathy's son Matthew died, I was preparing to speak at a retreat on the topic of encouragement, specifically the blessing and power in writing notes of encouragement. When Kathy found out that I was speaking on this topic, she emphatically told me that I had to tell women the importance of sending notes and letters to one another, *especially* to people who have experienced loss. I asked her to write down why this means so much to her:

"Whenever I receive a card or note, it touches an aching void in my soul. A sister has touched me with a piece of love that I didn't think or know I needed . . . *it was a gift of love that reached deep inside to a place that Jesus knew needed to be touched.*"

Take the time today to write a note or an e-mail and tell your friend how much she means to you.

By Asking

One sure way to let your friends in is by letting them know when you have a need. It could be as simple as asking if you could borrow a dress for an upcoming party or calling to see if they have a minute because you just need to vent. It could be an emergency like watching your kids so you can go to the hospital to be with a sick relative, or even letting them know that you're not feeling one hundred percent and you could use a hand with the kids. . . . There really is something special about the nurturing touch of a woman when you are down.

My girlfriend Nancy told me that she hadn't been feeling well all week but that it took about five days of being sick with the stomach flu to realize just how depleted she was. Nancy, like most women, was more aware of her family's needs than of her own, and so each day she kept rallying—thinking that her illness was going away—only to find that the next day she was feeling worse. Nancy didn't ask her teenage daughters for help, and she had a hard time going to her husband for much nurturing. By Saturday she was feeling resentful and beyond empty. Nancy talked to me about how much she misses her mom when she gets sick like this (her mom passed away a few years prior). I said, "I'd like to be there for you, Nancy . . . I'd bring you some 7-Up and saltines." Nancy's voice got really quiet. "I have a hard time thinking that anybody would want to drive all the way over to my house to help me." I asked her, "If I was sick and called you, would you want to help me?" In a moment of realization Nancy said, "Of course, I'd love to be there for you."

I know that it's challenging to reach out when you're down. You truly need the Lord to help you gain the courage and the boldness needed to reach out *with words* and then to open yourself up to receive the help God provides through a friend.

With Actions

**Dear children, let us not love with words or tongue
but with actions and in truth.**

(1 John 3:18)

We stumbled in the door following our summer vacation and discovered a bouquet of flowers on the counter and a lively little note from my neighbor Michele that read:

WELCOME HOME!
We missed you sooo much.
There are fresh milk, apples, bread, bananas, and a chicken in the fridge.
See you soon!
Love, the Bracketts

This simple *action* from our neighbors communicated such love to our family.

Show Her You Know Her

I think that one of the most fun ways to love your friend with action is to do things for her that communicate that you know her. In order to do this you have to be observant and take the time to tuck away those little tidbits of information you discover along the way. Things like her favorite:

- Color
- Food (snacks, Starbucks, dessert, dinner, restaurant)
- Music
- Scent (cologne, candle, lotion)
- Author
- Movie
- Scripture verse/theme

You can also take note of her sense of style (whether fashion or home décor), her sense of humor (does she think *Seinfeld* is funny or is she more of an *I Love Lucy* fan?), and her sense of adventure.

Once you begin to get to know your friend, you can surprise her with actions and little gifts that communicate this.

One year we threw our girlfriend Andrea a mini birthday party that communicated that we knew her. We had a grown-up slumber party at my house. We rented *Legends of the Fall,* the only Brad Pitt (her favorite actor) movie she had not yet seen, we ordered her favorite salad, I made her favorite cookies, and we laughed the night away. (After the movie ended, of course—I mean, how tragic can one movie be, for goodness' sake?) The highlight was the surprise video that her mom was gracious enough to lend us, which featured Andrea as an eighteen-year-old beauty pageant contestant. Her mom was also kind enough to let us borrow the teal one-shouldered satin gown that she'd worn in the pageant, which Andrea modeled for us.

It was a great birthday, and Andrea felt loved and known, which was of course our goal.

Helping your friend feel known need not be extravagant or expensive. It could be as simple as tearing a recipe out of a magazine for her because it looks like something she would like to make. It could be e-mailing her a funny joke, calling and telling her you were thinking of her because her favorite song was playing on the radio, or leaving her a card to let her know that you remembered the anniversary of the passing of one of her loved ones.

Life is busy, and I'm sure there are many times when a friend has come to mind and you thought something like: *I need to give her a call, drop her a note, bring her a gift . . .* but then you forget about it. I encourage you to ask the Lord to help you to stop and write that note or write a note to yourself as a reminder to love your friend with action. It is a small but powerful way to put feet to your prayers and connect with your friend.

Here are some ideas of ways you can connect with action:

- Send a note of encouragement when your friend is feeling down.
- Make a meal for a friend (or let someone cook for you) during a time of stress (surgery/sickness, death in the family, or just a bad day).
- Put together a care package for a friend who is traveling.
- Throw a celebration party (birthday, anniversary, job offer).
- Bake her favorite dessert and let her know that "she makes life so much sweeter!"
- Leave her a little gift on her porch.

Presence: "Showing Up" for the Big and Little Things

Stay is a charming word in a friend's vocabulary.[4]

—Louisa May Alcott

Life is made up of big milestones and little moments. Friends who show up for both are friends whose hearts are knit together. Your presence matters. If your gut tells you to go, even if your friend hasn't asked you to come, I encourage you to show up. We can all look back on the defining moments in our lives and recall the circle that surrounded us.

There are times when I didn't ask my friends to show up and they did anyway; one example is at my grandpa's funeral. I have a difficult time describing what it felt like to look around the church and see so many familiar faces—people who had never even met my grandpa, but because they loved me they showed up. I have internalized their presence and it remains with me still, eight years later.

Milestones and moments that you don't want to miss:

- Births
- Deaths
- Birthdays
- Weddings
- Vow renewals
- Graduations
- Baptisms, confirmations, and dedications
- Retirement parties
- Illnesses or injuries
- Children's milestones

My sister Nancy was a single mom for over a decade, and the friends who showed up for the big and little moments in her life during those years truly showed her the love of Christ in countless ways:

> I was a single mom for ten years, and my friends were my true support . . . especially my friend Leslie, who is still a single mom. . . . Since I didn't have a spouse to process with, I would talk to my friends Katie and Leslie daily, sometimes several times a day if there was a pressing issue. Both of them were so vital to me in that they did the things a spouse would

do: give hugs, encouragement, help with projects like painting the restaurant before I opened it, and major shopping trips like to Costco. With Leslie, since we were across-the-street neighbors and had boys who were close in age, it was like we each had two houses.

On Saturdays we would walk across the street in our pj's (all of us) to eat breakfast at whoever's house had the eggs and the half and half. The kids would play, we would process . . . lament, laugh, and swap advice. When one of us had a hard day or was exhausted or PMS-ing, one of us would take both boys while the other took a nap, a shower, or just zoned out for a few hours. Katie and I would lament our singlehood, try to meet our spouses through friends, church, or the Internet (worked for me but not for her), and talk about God. I helped her with teaching, she helped me with my walk. . . . If we had all been married our friendships would not have been as rich. We told each other things we would have told our husbands, and we did things for each other that our spouses would have done. God set it up that way, though, since the time we shared before we got married cemented us all together.

Spending Intentional Time Together

My girlfriend Heather and I are HUGE fans of the Women of Faith conferences and have attended them together for the last decade. Our most memorable conference was the one we road-tripped to. We bought tickets to the San Jose conference (a five-hour drive from our home in Los Angeles), called up Grandma Harriet (my husband's 95-year-old grandma), who lived in the area, to tell her we were coming, packed up the minivan, and took off. The hours flew by as we gabbed, sang worship songs together, and ate junk food. Before we knew it we were picking up Grandma Harriet for a trip to her favorite Mexican restaurant. The weekend was fabulous not only because of the conference, but because of the extended amount of time my friend and I got to spend one-on-one. There's nothing like the special ingredient of time to weave hearts together.

Schedule some time to be with your friends:

- Plan a trip that you can look forward to—even one night away will bless you!
- Make a frozen yogurt date.
- Go scrapbooking.
- Go out to dinner.
- Schedule a day at the spa.

Many of my friends are across country, so I have to be creative. Besides phone calls and fun little e-mail exchanges, I plan weekend vacations. Gena and I recently went to Tampa, Florida, for two nights and three days, and simply sat poolside and chatted for hours. Then we ordered in and watched sappy romantic comedies. It was such a great getaway and a needed "Gena-fix" for me. We need our friends, and it's so crucial that we invest time, money, whatever it takes, into those friendships.

—Michelle Medlock Adams, author of 33 books, including
Divine Stories of the Yahweh Sisterhood

Prayer

Sometimes our prayers for our friends are the greatest gifts we can give them.[5]

I was driving down Wilshire Boulevard, in Southern California, on a bright, sunny day. As my car slowed to round a curve in the road, I caught sight of two elderly women standing on the sidewalk. One was holding an umbrella (or is it a parasol when used on a sunny day?) with one hand and the other was gently resting on the neck of her friend. She was securing her friend within the shade of the umbrella, shielding her from the hot sun. They were smiling, talking animatedly, while I drove by with a big smile on my face.

This image reminds me of a special privilege we have in friendship: prayer. Prayer connects hearts like nothing else I know. When we pray for our friends we are drawing them into the presence of our heavenly Father, shielding them from the evils of the world, loving them by holding them close in spirit.

There have been times in my life when I have found it too difficult even to utter a prayer for myself, times when I felt like I could not last another day. On those days I knew my friends were holding me up in prayer; they were going to the Father for me and in so doing were bringing me into the presence of love, peace, and joy.

Whether you are praying for your friend privately or giving her a big hug and praying right then and there, I encourage you to keep your friend(s) in your prayers and allow her to do the same for you. I guarantee the Lord will use this action to connect your hearts. Here is what prayer did in the life of one woman who attended a weekly prayer meeting of her Moms In Touch group:

> **What a life-changer attending Moms In Touch has been for me. . . . At Moms In Touch I hear the concerns of my heart expressed by other moms who voice their concerns, sentiments, humility, and yearnings to our Lord in prayer. . . . I awaken on Mondays happily knowing I am going to this prayer meeting where I will be rejuvenated and recharged with a renewed sense of closeness to Christ and to my sisters in Christ. These sisters always humbly and often humorously share, through prayer, the challenges they face while raising their children. Women whom I would not otherwise have taken the time to know I am now drawn to because of the comfort found in our common prayers. We have gotten to know each other and our children by expressing in prayer our commonly held faults, needs, shortcomings, love, happiness, and ambitions. Last year I began an evening family prayer time in our home during Lent. My husband and I loved it so much we have continued on. This would not have happened if I had not been attending Moms In Touch. My family life is stronger and I am soldiering on more diligently.**
>
> —Catherine P. MacAdam, co-founder of Agua Dulce Vineyards

They all joined together constantly in prayer.

(Acts 1:14)

Actions to Avoid
(They Tear the Chain Apart)

Isolating Yourself

**Let us not give up meeting together, as some are in the
habit of doing, but let us encourage one another—and all
the more as you see the Day approaching.**

(Hebrews 10:25)

In the first few years of having close friendships I had a habit of
isolating and withdrawing myself. It was a coping mechanism that I
had formed when I was growing up—the best way I knew to protect
my heart. God began to show me that I no longer needed to protect
my heart in this way, and I began to learn to communicate with my
friends and to hang in there when things got tough or I started feeling depressed or unsure of myself. To be honest, it is still an area
that I have to pray about and move out in. The blessing is that God
surrounded me with people who were more mature than I in this
area. I still remember a day when I was isolating myself and one of
my friends showed up on my doorstep with a card that said: "I know
things are awkward right now, but I want you to know I'm not going
anywhere. . . . I'm committed to our friendship."

Now when I begin to feel a desire to withdraw, I have learned to
let my friends know by saying something like "I don't even want to
be with me, and I can't believe that you gals want to be with me!" It's
been helpful to let them in, and it's also been helpful to ask them if
they wouldn't mind initiating with me for a little while (with a phone
call here and there or just showing up at my house) until my desire
to isolate dissipates.

In times of grief we are apt to hear dark voices—voices
that tell us we are no longer people of value, beloved by
God. If we withdraw from friends—a common response
to depression—then those voices have no competition. We need to be with compassionate women who
will come alongside us and show us that we are lovable
human beings, precious in God's sight and in their sight.
If our friends don't come to be with us we must
take the initiative to ask for their company.[6]

—Dee Brestin

Gossip

To speak ill of others is a dishonest way of praising ourselves; let us be above such transparent egotism. If you
can't say good and encouraging things, say nothing.
Nothing is often a good thing to do, and
always a clever thing to say.[7]

—Will Durant

He who covers over an offense promotes love, but
whoever repeats the matter separates close friends.

(Proverbs 17:9)

I heard a pastor recently say that you know you're gossiping if you
have to change the subject or stop talking when the person about
whom you were just speaking comes walking in. Gossip is one of those
actions that tears at the very fabric of friendship. I approached one
of my writing buddies, Shirley, about the topic of gossip because I
know it is a subject she feels strongly about. She writes:

My first memories of gossip are from my childhood and
seeing certain neighbors on their porches talking. The
only talking being done, of course, was about the other
neighbors. As we got older, they'd make us kids go play
somewhere else so that we couldn't hear them. . . .
My mother was never a part of it, though, and I don't
remember ever hearing my mother gossip. . . . On one
occasion, I remember a neighbor asking my mom if she
could borrow some money. My dad later told us kids:

**"They asked your mom for the money because they
knew she wouldn't tell anyone. . . ." It was a proud moment for me, and I remember wanting to be that way
too. They may have gossiped about her (and others)
openly, but inside they knew my mom's character, and
ultimately the Lord knows too, and that's all that matters.
That memory helps me on a regular basis.**

I love what Shirley wrote because it emphasizes the fact that we
are not only hurting friendships when we participate in gossip, but
we are modeling a lack of integrity to those around us—especially
to children. We are teaching them what is okay and what is not.
Shirley's mother passed away when Shirley was a little girl, and yet
the integrity that her mother displayed in this seemingly small way
continues to affect her to this day and influences the way she chooses
to raise her own children.

Unless you have permission to share personal information with
another friend, do your absolute best to keep information to yourself.
Even if it is being shared in the form of a prayer request, it is still *not*
your information to share unless permission has been granted. *Gossip is a sure way to disconnect what you have been working to bind together.*
Ask the Lord to "set a guard over [your] mouth" (Psalm 141:3) on
a regular basis.

Another thing to pray about and to be careful of that falls under the
category of gossip is speaking negatively about other people, places, or
activities for any reason. Sometimes we justify ourselves or decisions we
have made by criticizing others. If you feel that you are being called
to make a certain decision, then make that decision and ask the Lord
to cause you to pause before you say more than you should.

**For out of the abundance of the heart the mouth speaks.
Every idle word men may speak, they will give account
of it in the day of judgment. For by your words you will
be justified, and by your words you will be condemned.**

(Matthew 12:34, 36-37 NKJV)

The tongue has the power of life and death.

(Proverbs 18:21)

Lessons From "The Greats"

Keep Confidences

> **Make sure that when a confidence is shared, it stays there. Many years ago, we promised to do this by going around the circle and touching our right thumbs together and repeating the words "in blood." What started out as playful symbolism is now, thirty plus years later, our tradition when we are sharing from the heart.**

Begin now to make keeping confidences your tradition in friendship.

Refusing to Receive Gifts

I observed a classic illustration of saying no to a gift this past Christmas. I was at a football practice for my son, and one of the moms had purchased beautiful cellophane-wrapped coffee cakes as gifts for a few of her football friends and their families. When she handed one to a friend, she refused it with an adamant "No, I'm not going to take it!" The other gals standing around looked at one another in astonishment. The giver said, "Come on, take it. It's for your family," to which the receiver replied, "You already gave us a gift, and I'm not taking it. I'd be the one who eats it!" Unruffled, the giver finally said, "Listen, you either take the cake, or I hit you over the head with it—and it's heavy!" We all laughed. The recipient laughed too, finally accepting the gift.

Now, while this was a lighthearted, funny moment, the symbolism is powerful. Let us not refuse to "take the cake" of extended love, support, and gifts our friends offer us. This is a sure way to damage or break the chain of connection.

The Pain of Rejection

According to John Eldredge, "The worst fear for a woman is abandonment. Like a man who refuses to play the man for fear of failing, a woman who shuns intimacy only reveals her fear of rejection by refusing to face it honestly, openly."[8]

School was out and my girlfriend and I walked side by side down our gravel road. When we got to my house, I continued on down the street toward my friend's house. She looked at me inquisitively and said "What are you doing?" I smiled and, thinking she would be excited, replied, "I'm going to your house today!" "Why?" she said, not a drop of enthusiasm in her voice. "Your dad told me that when I finished the books he gave me, I could come over and borrow some more." (When my girlfriend's father, a teacher, found out that I hadn't learned how to read yet, he had lent me the first few "Dick and Jane" books.) "You *did not* finish them yet!" My friend said, her voice rising angrily. By this time we had stopped walking and stood in the middle of the quiet street. Bewildered, I replied, "I did . . . really." "Well you're NOT coming to my house!" my friend hollered, and with that she turned on her heel and ran as fast as she could to her house. After a while I continued slowly in the direction of my friend's house. I climbed the three cement steps and knocked on the cold metallic screen door. Her mom answered, one arm around her daughter's heaving shoulders. My friend's face was wet with tears as she gulped air trying to say "I'm sorry." Her mom handed me the books and said, "We will see you tomorrow, honey." I walked back home, knowing in my gut that I must have done something really horrible. I didn't know what it was, but I was sure it was awful.

When I was writing about connecting in friendship, this memory kept coming to my mind and I wasn't sure why. The more I prayed about it the more clarity I got. I think there are times we "miss" each other in friendship. Times when we are showing love to our friend and our love gets rejected, or times when someone is trying to do something for us and we don't want to have anything to do with it. When I think of not letting somebody in (refusing to receive love or turning our back on connection), this is the picture that comes to my mind: two little girls who love each other dearly but are somehow missing each other.

71

I look back now and know that during that period in my friend's life, her parents were on the brink of divorce. With that perspective, I can only imagine that a six-year-old girl did not want anyone or anything else coming between her and her daddy, nor did she want any more surprises, even if it was a friend saying she was going to come over for a minute. I know that now, but I did not know it then. I only knew the pain of rejection and the pain of a friend communicating "I don't want you, and I don't want you to come over."

I tell this story for two reasons. First of all, I think we all need to grow in our awareness of one another. We need to recognize that there are pains or wounds in the friend who refuses to receive connection as well as in the friend who feels her love is being rejected.

For the friend who is not letting love in, there might be a fear of being abandoned (so she only lets people in so far), or perhaps she has been betrayed by someone close to her and is desperately trying to keep history from repeating itself, or maybe she just doesn't feel that she is worthy of being loved. Whether she is aware of it or not, when a friend is not allowing herself to be loved, she is in pain and in need of grace and healing.

There is also pain on the side of the giver who feels rejected. Perhaps she feels that her love isn't good enough or that she's not "doing it right" or that she deserves to be rejected. She is in need of acknowledgment, affirmation, and love.

I think too that more often than not we take interactions too personally. Just like as a little girl I tried to figure out what I did to bring on the reaction I got from my friend, we can stand in the middle of the street and ask, "What did *I do* wrong?"

While introspection has its place, try to keep in mind that it is probably not all about you. Bring your feelings of rejection and hurt to the Lord in prayer and keep in mind that your heavenly Father will always receive you, that the love you give is good, and that His Son Jesus knows the pain of the rejection you are experiencing, and He is able to comfort you. Once you have dealt with your feelings of rejection, try to replace your questions of "What did I do wrong?" or

"What's her problem?" (hear the sarcastic undertones?) with "Lord, what is going on with my friend that would cause her to react in this way?" and even deeper, "Lord, heal her wounded heart and help me know if there is a way I can minister to her."

There are times when God will use interactions such as these to close a door. He could be letting you know that this is *not* a relationship, for the time being, that He wants you to invest in. Pray about this as well. He may be letting you know this is not a person that is ready for a mutual friendship. In Proverbs 4:23 we are admonished, "Above all else, guard your heart, for it is the wellspring of life." Ask God for discernment with your friendships and, once you have His guidance, continue to reach out to women with your love and with your life.

> **And so I have come to understand that strength, inner strength, comes from receiving love as much as it comes from giving it. . . . God's love will never change us if we don't accept it.[9]**
>
> —Donald Miller

 ## Ponder

If you had to choose, what are you more comfortable with: the act of giving or the act of receiving? Why is this?

Can you think of an occasion when a friend showed her love for you with an action? What were the circumstances surrounding this?

Which friendship(s) are you currently a part of that you would consider mutual?

When was the last time you found yourself withdrawing or isolating yourself?

How have you been wounded by gossip? What were the circumstances?

What do you do when you find yourself involved in gossip (passively listening or actively participating)?

Why do you think gossip is such a temptation for women?

Did you find yourself stuck anywhere in this chapter? Did you find a place that needs the healing touch of God or the strength and courage to move forward?

 ## Pray

Lord, one of the things I want most in life is to take your love in and give your love out. I thank you for showing me that one of the channels this is likely to occur through is friendship. Please help me to receive your love extended to me through the hand of another. I confess that I feel _____ (tell the Lord any feelings that arise when you think through this concept; for example, uncomfortable receiving things, suspicious of motives). *Make me aware, moment by moment, when you are trying to love me in this way so that I don't miss it. Please help me move out when you call me to extend love to another. Help me connect with my friends and potential friends in ways that are meaningful and heartfelt, and please help these friends receive my love as a gift from you. Thank you for friendship, Lord.*

 ## Apply

Connecting With the Daisies in Your Chain

The next time you get sick, let your friends know (especially if you need something).

Start brainstorming with your friends about doing a road trip.

Simply say "thank you" the next time a friend offers you a gift or a compliment.

Keep a picture of your friend(s) in a prime location in your home, and every time you see it say a prayer for her.

Buy a book, read it, and then pass it around your "daisy chain." Here are some suggestions to get you started:

Tuesdays With Morrie by Mitch Albom

After Anne by Roxanne Henke

THE SISTER CHICKS series by Robin Jones Gunn

Redeeming Love by Francine Rivers

Letters From a Friend

To My Fellow Football Mom,

We have been together in the heat and in the cold; on hard metal seats and uncomfortable folding chairs. We have done drills together, been yelled at together, eaten junk food on the sidelines together, and driven to games together. We have shared recipes, stories, and jokes. We have screamed together, laughed together, and cried together. We have worried together, cheered together, and even prayed together. We share the common bond of a love for our kids and enjoyment of the game of football.

Please accept my heartfelt thanks for all that you have done for my child . . . you have kept him hydrated, you have made beautiful banners every week for him to run through at the end of the game, you made sure there were snacks, fruits, and drinks at each game so he wouldn't pass out, you have blown horns and applauded for him when he made a big play, you have decorated your car in support of his team, you have sprayed him down when it was hot and covered him up when it was cold, you have loved him with your words and with your actions, and for this I am eternally grateful.

We have been a family for the last six months, and I consider it an honor, a privilege, and a blessing to have been at your side this football season. You are a wonderful, loving woman, and your family is blessed to have you in their lives . . . if they forget to tell you that in the future, have them give me a call and after I give them a talking to I will remind them what a priceless gift you are—a woman who is worthy of respect and love.

Your Forever Football Friend,
Tracy

Chapter 5

Handling the Flowers

In the process of connecting the flowers and wearing the crown, make sure to use a gentle touch so as not to crush or destroy the chain.

From the fullness of his grace we have all received one blessing after another. For the law was given through Moses; grace and truth came through Jesus Christ.

(John 1:16–17)

I have friends with whom I can laugh; friends who bring youth and adventure/play into my life; friends whom I can trust with my pearls, who will pray for me, who will give me the *love and truth* I need at the moment. What I see now that I hadn't when I was younger, is that each woman in my life has been *woven there by my God and brings blessings to me from Him.* My prayer in this is that I may be the blessing to these women that they have been to me.

—Nancy S.

My stomach was churning. I needed to tell her; I needed to let her know that I wasn't moving (as we had planned), to tell her that I was letting her down. My heart was pounding, my eyes watering, and my mouth was suddenly as dry as the Sudan.

We sat on the couch and I don't recall how I started. Actually, I don't remember much except that somehow I told my friend that I would not be moving to San Francisco as we had planned but that I would be moving to Nevada and going back to school. She looked at me for a moment, and then without missing a beat she said, "That's okay, you shouldn't move to San Francisco if you don't feel certain about it. Don't worry about me, Tracy, I needed a change anyway." With those words I felt the nausea dissipate, my pulse slow down, and a remarkable sense of relief and gratitude rise along with a bucketful of tears.

Beth had every right to be absolutely furious with me. After all, I was the one who had come up with the idea of leaving Southern California and heading up north to get an apartment together. I had sold her on the fun we'd have teaching and competing in aerobics together at the prestigious clubs of Northern California. And now, at the eleventh hour, I was leaving her high and dry. But instead of the anticipated angry response, I was getting grace handed to me.

Grace is defined as "an undeserved favor or gift; the undeserved forgiveness, kindness, and mercy that God gives us."[1]

Grace is what Jesus gave us when He died on the cross for our sins. He lived a perfect life and chose to give us a holy exchange: our sin for His righteousness. Have you ever noticed that you don't get grace until you realize you need grace? I didn't get grace for a long time because I worked really hard not to need it. I worked at following the rules: Be a good person, be a good friend, and keep your promises. This moment with my friend Beth was a glimpse of grace. I wasn't following the rules (for I was certainly letting her down), and yet she gave me love, acceptance, and support.

In order to have growing friendships we must handle our daisies gently—with grace, truth, and a light touch. If we are too rough with our crown of flowers we can easily crush and destroy it, and if we hold on too tightly to our crown of flowers we can even cause our own hands to bleed.

How are you doing in the grace department? Do you know that you are a sinner saved by grace alone? Does that translate to your relationships, specifically to your friendships? For example, how well do you do when it comes to forgiving a friend for hurting you, letting you down, or not being everything that you need? How do you do when you are the one who does the hurting or the letting down? Do you have grace for yourself? How do you do when you are trying to work out differences in your relationship?

Grace

Working It Out

Understand Your Basic Personality Differences

Marita Littauer, a personalities expert and author of more than nineteen books, including *Wired That Way,* has this to say about growing friendships:

> **Some relationships work more naturally than others; for example, when a sanguine (one of the personality types) says she's made a new best friend it is because she has just met someone who is her same personality type. She has met another sanguine and they just clicked. . . . That's not to say that every flower in your crown should be the same personality type as you. A crown of friendship that holds many *different kinds of personalities* will bring more richness to your life. *It may take more work, but it is worth the effort.***

I believe that when we have a basic understanding of the personality types, we have a greater likelihood of appreciating one another's strengths and extending grace for one another's weaknesses. When we see that an individual is simply wired in a different way than we are, we can love them more effectively because we see that their emotional needs are different than our own, and we're less likely to personalize their behavior. (For example, "She is trying to be disrespectful to me by showing up late to all of our get-togethers" versus "She is a sanguine, and being disorganized or late is one of the weaknesses of her personality.")

Here is a *brief* overview of the personalities.[2] If you would like more information on this topic, including the test to discover what personality type you are, pick up a copy of *Wired That Way* by Marita and Florence Littauer.

Personality Overviews

Popular Sanguines—"Let's do it the fun way."
Desire: to have fun

Key strengths: ability to talk about anything at any time at any place, bubbling personality, optimism, sense of humor, storytelling ability, enjoyment of people

Key weaknesses: disorganized, can't remember details or names, exaggerates, not serious about anything, trusts others to do the work, too gullible and naïve

Emotional needs: attention, affection, approval, acceptance

Recognized by their: constant talking, loud volume, bright eyes

Powerful Cholerics—"Let's do it my way."
Desire: to have control

Key strengths: ability to take charge of anything instantly and to make quick, correct judgments

Key weaknesses: too bossy, domineering, autocratic, insensitive, impatient, unwilling to delegate or give credit to others

Emotional needs: sense of obedience, appreciation for accomplishments, credit for ability

Recognized by their: fast-moving approach, quick grab for control, self-confidence, restless and overpowering attitude

Perfect Melancholies—"Let's do it the right way."
Desire: to have it right

Key strengths: ability to organize and set long-range goals, have high standards and ideals, analyze deeply

Key weaknesses: easily depressed, too much time on preparation, too focused on details, remembers negatives, suspicious of others

Emotional needs: sense of stability, space, silence, sensitivity, support

Recognized by their: serious and sensitive nature, well-mannered approach, self-deprecating comments, meticulous and well-groomed looks

Peaceful Phlegmatics—"Let's do it the easy way."

Desire: to avoid conflict, keep peace

Key strengths: balance, even disposition, dry sense of humor, pleasing personality

Key weaknesses: lack of decisiveness, enthusiasm, and energy; a hidden will of iron

Emotional needs: sense of respect, feeling of worth, understanding, emotional support

Recognized by their: calm approach, relaxed posture (sitting or leaning when possible)

Taking Responsibility

At one of our first Monday night meetings my friend Liz decided she was going to leave early. We had decided as a group that we would meet from 8:00–9:30 p.m. Yet after what I perceived to be a very short time, Liz started gathering her things together to leave. I said something like, "What are you doing? I thought we'd all decided to set aside ninety minutes to be together?" Liz looked flustered and Andrea came to Liz's defense and said, "Oh Liz, don't listen to Tracy.

She's just a 'more' girl." She was insinuating that I was never satisfied and always wanted more.

Now, Liz and I worked this out and are still close to this day, but the reason I share the story is because of what Andrea said. The next Monday when we got together I brought up her comment and the fact that I didn't really appreciate what she said about me. Without missing a beat Andrea said, "Yeah, I'm sorry. I *was* trying to hurt you." It was like someone had opened a door and allowed a fresh breeze to come blowing in. I had never in my life seen someone take responsibility for their actions like that. It was so helpful, so healing.

If you are working things out in a friendship, I recommend that you take *ownership* and *responsibility* for as much as you are aware of. By doing so you are not saying, "It's all my fault," but rather that you care enough to see your friend and that you're willing to take a good look at yourself.

We can do this when we know that we are loved enough by God and secure enough in His love through Christ that we can ask the Spirit: "Search me, O God, and know my heart; test me and know my anxious thoughts. See if there is any offensive way in me, and lead me in the way everlasting" (Psalm 139: 23–24).

Asking for and Extending Forgiveness

Be kind and compassionate to one another, forgiving each other, just as in Christ God forgave you.

(Ephesians 4:32)

My daughter and I were doing a Wal-Mart run the other day when we bumped into one of her best friends. As soon as the girls saw each other their faces lit up and they started waving frantically and smiling from ear to ear. As we made our way up and down the aisles of the store, Grace caught a glimpse of Allie's long brown hair and so she jumped into the aisle, waved frantically one more time, and shouted, "Hi, Allie!" Allie turned, got a goofy grin on her face, and waved back. As my daughter turned toward me she smiled and said quietly to herself, "I just love her."

There will be times in our friendships when we need to work out our differences, forgive one another, or simply hang in there when things get awkward. When these times come, it is important to remember the love we have for one another. It is important to recall the beautiful and excellent qualities of our friend and the warm memories that we have experienced together. It is imperative to dwell on the fact that she too is a child of God and that there was a time when your face lit up when you saw her and you said to yourself, "I just love her." It is imperative to dwell on the fact that when you've made a mess of things your heavenly Father continues to tell you that He loves you, forgives you, and that you cause His face to "radiate with joy" (Numbers 6:24 TLB).

Asking a friend to forgive you is different than apologizing to her. Saying a heartfelt "I'm sorry" is of great value but even more vulnerable and healing is saying "I am sorry; I know that I hurt you (by doing _____); would you please forgive me?" You are waiting in humility for her to extend you forgiveness.

When we are the individual being asked to forgive an offense and we discover that we are having a difficult time doing so, we need to examine why that is. Why do we want to hang on to the offense? Is it to punish the individual? To have a reason to ignore her or no longer have a relationship with her? I am not recommending we beat ourselves up for not forgiving a person. But I do think it is *very important* that a *lack of forgiveness act as a red flag* to point us to Christ, who can help us understand why it is we would choose bitterness over freedom.

I also believe that we can only truly forgive if we are aware of having been truly forgiven. In John 15:12-13, Jesus says, "My command is this: Love each other as I have loved you. Greater love has no one than this, that he lay down his life for his friends." Jesus loved us by dying for us, voluntarily laying His life down for us. Dwell on that for a moment . . . are you aware that you needed Him to do that for you? Are you aware that your sin needed to be covered, forgiven? When we take the time to remember all that we have been forgiven, extending forgiveness becomes a little more doable, doesn't it? God would not call us to do something that He would not help us do, and He calls us to forgive. He calls us to lay down our bitterness and our anger, and as an act of our will say, "I choose to forgive you."

Recording artist Kathy Troccoli says of a time she was wounded by her friend and coauthor Dee Brestin: "I had to forgive her, because I've broken confidences in other friendships. Part of the process is realizing we're all capable of doing hurtful things. So you go back to the bottom line and ask yourself, *Even though my friend has hurt me, does she love me?* And I absolutely knew Dee loved me. Because of that, we were able to move on."[3]

Truth

Then you will know the truth, and
the truth will set you free.

(John 8:32)

Over the years I have come full circle in what kind of a friend I long to be and what kind of a friend I look for. When I was much younger I liked having many friends—different ages, different backgrounds, different dynamics. I have a very outgoing personality and make friends easily. I have been known to make friends in the grocery store checkout line or at the post office. But I have learned a great deal over the years, and one of those things is that the main component—the one that means the most to me—is a spiritual connection.

—Sheri Torelli, author

Growing in Truth Together

Now you can have real love for everyone because your souls have been cleansed from selfishness and hatred when you trusted Christ to save you; so see to it that you really do love each other warmly, with all your hearts.

(1 Peter 1:22 TLB)

Yesterday was a scheduled writing day for me, which meant that the kids took the carpool to school and I stayed in my best writing clothes (my pajamas), climbed up onto my bed, spread out all of my writing paraphernalia (papers, books, several translations of the Bible, pens, and snacks), pulled the computer onto my lap, and got to work. About one hour into writing, I got the call from school every mother dreads: "Your daughter isn't feeling well." "I'll be right there," I replied quickly as I leaped out of the bed. Within minutes I'd traded my pj's for sweats and was flying down the road praying that Grace would be okay until I got there. God answered my prayers, and while she was in a lot of discomfort, she waited until we got home to . . . well, you know.

My scheduled writing day was quickly transformed into a "take care of my little one day." I was thankful I was home and that my schedule is such that I can take care of my kids in moments like these. I was thankful up until this morning, when I realized that I have only ten days left to finish this book.

Panic began to settle around me like fog on a misty morning. It was time to look to *God's truth,* and as usual He met me right where I needed Him to: "Fear not, for I am with you; be not dismayed, for I am your God. *I will* strengthen you, yes, *I will* help you, *I will* uphold you with My righteous right hand. . . . I, the Lord your God, *will* hold your right hand" (Isaiah 41:10, 13 NKJV, emphasis mine). As I read these truths I was reminded that it is with my right hand that I write. I then turned to a devotional and read that "no earthly circumstances can hinder the fulfillment of God's Word. We must look steadfastly at His immutable Word and not at the uncertainty of this ever-changing world."[4]

Once again God's truth saved the day! No matter how things look, no matter how things around me change, God remains the same, and He will keep His Word. If God was able to create the universe in seven days, He is certainly able to help me finish my book in the next ten. I need to keep looking to His Truth instead of my reality, and I need to continue to remind myself and my friends that the

God we serve keeps His promises, and His truth is solid ground on which to stand.

After ten years of facilitating women's Bible studies, I have observed that as women gather together to pore over God's Word, new friendships are formed and existing ones are deepened. We are experiencing God's truth and grace through these growing friendships.

—Jennifer

Helping One Another Recognize the Liar and His Lies

The only way you can be discerning about the lies of the enemy is to stand firm in God's truth. When you are standing firm in truth you not only begin to have more personal victory, you can start to help your friends experience more victory.

It's been helpful to have a friend alert me to the fact that I am in the midst of a spiritual attack or to help me recognize the voice of the deceiver. Just the other day I was having dinner with girlfriends, and I was telling them how in the process of writing this book I was often hearing critical voices in my head: "Who are you to be writing a book?" and "You think people are actually going to care what you think?" My friend Shirley said point blank, "That's the Enemy." She then proceeded to do a demonstration of what she does when she hears those voices. She looks over her shoulder, and with a light swipe of her hand (as if she were brushing off lint), and in her terrific New York accent, she says, "Get outta heeah!"

I laughed hard when she demonstrated her technique. I love that she made the voices little by brushing them off as if they were mere annoyances. And that's what they are when we recall the truth of God's Word:

You, dear children, are from God and have overcome them, because the one who is in you is greater than the one who is in the world.

(1 John 4:4)

Say No to Denial

It appears that genuine friendship cannot possibly exist where one of the parties is unwilling to hear the truth and the other equally indisposed to speak it.[5]

—Cicero

God's truth is not the only kind of truth we need to bring to our friendships in order for them to grow. We need to bring the truth of our feelings, our thoughts, and our whole selves to the relationship. Some personalities are more natural at this than others (choleric and melancholy), and these people might benefit from erring on the side of being more discerning about when their truths need to be told. Other personalities need to be more honest about their feelings, thoughts, and opinions (phlegmatics and sanguines). These friends need to realize that not telling the truth, not working it out, and avoiding conflict can lead to *distance* in a relationship.

Sometimes we can get our feelings hurt and minimize the fact by thinking, *It's not that big a deal* or *She probably didn't even mean anything by it.* But then we may realize over time that we are still hanging on to the offense and even adding to it. This lack of truth telling can lead to strains in the relationship. Listen to how it affected Lorna:

I've had one close friend who would keep everything inside and pretend things were always fine. But then at some point she would explode with all this built-up stuff. It is much easier for everyone to handle the stuff bit by bit along the way instead of all at once, every couple of years. . . . I was so hurt by the avalanche of words that it was some time before we were both able to grow past it and decide the friendship was worth the effort. We also had to learn to communicate more clearly. We were roommates at the time, so there was no place to run, so to speak. The good news is that after working it out we are still friends twenty-four years later.

Sometimes the truths we need to speak can be as simple as confessing, "You hurt my feelings when you said . . ."

"I need a shoulder to cry on right now, not solutions to my problems."

"Can you call me more often? I feel like I am doing all the initiating in this relationship and it makes me feel like I am not a priority to you."

"I am angry because . . ."

For those who tend to avoid conflict and want everybody to like them, this can be challenging. The thing to remember is that telling the truth in a friendship has the potential of communicating: *I care enough about you and want you to know me enough that I will risk telling you how I feel.*

I have learned how to communicate difficult feelings to a friend and learned to follow the Lord. Through this the Lord taught me that I am stronger than I thought I was.

—Patti

"Danger!"

Wounds from a friend can be trusted, but an enemy multiplies kisses.

(Proverbs 27:6)

Have you ever wished one of your friends would have pulled you aside, given you a tender shake, and asked you that all-important question "What are you thinking?"

Soon after graduating from college I became romantically involved with my boss, who was several years my senior. In my one great act of rebellion (from the previously mentioned shiny, "good girl" image), I moved in with him and so began a destructive cycle of behavior. It ultimately ended with my dad (per my request) driving thirteen hours from Reno to San Diego to load me, my Jeep, and all of my stuff onto a truck and turn around and drive me thirteen hours home that same day.

I look back on this time of my life as the time I became aware of my sinfulness. Through this one major detour down rebellion lane, my eyes were opened to my intense need of a Savior. For this I will always be grateful, because if I hadn't seen my sin I wouldn't have seen God's grace. That being said, I do look back and wonder why the friends and family in my life did not ask me what I was thinking, or scream, "Danger!" and warn me that I was headed in the wrong direction (and a dangerous one at that).

I also wonder what I would have done if one of these friends *had* risked telling me the "truth in love" (Ephesians 4:15). In all likelihood I would have felt offended or judged and quite possibly have even distanced myself from the relationship with that person. But I think (and hope) that in the long run I would have felt loved—loved enough to have had a friend risk our friendship in order to help me. When I feel that God is calling me to speak a difficult truth to a friend, I can think back to this time and gain courage. Since I tend to be more of a grace person, it helps me to remember that there are times when *speaking the truth is the most loving thing to do.*

Truth can be tricky. I have heard it said that "people don't care how much you know until they know how much you care." People want to *know* you love them. They want to *know* you are for them, and they want to *know* that you are with them before you start telling them about their blind spots or their brokenness. My pastor likens it to surgery: If you need a cancer taken out, you need a lot of anesthesia (grace) before you can have it cut out with the knife (of truth).[6]

I remember getting a phone call from a friend who had been struggling in her marriage for quite a long time. She was just letting me know that she was choosing to leave the marriage. This is a woman whom I had prayed for and with, and whose marriage and children I had prayed for. I was heartbroken, as I'm sure she was. She certainly didn't need my permission or my blessing to make this decision, nor did I possess the power to bestow either of these things on her. I could only in as loving a way as possible let her know that in light of God's truth and her situation, I didn't think she was doing the right thing but that I would continue to pray for her and pray for the reconciliation of her family.

> **There are times when we must speak up. If we make the mistake of quietly empathizing when we should be alerting our friend to danger, we may actually be holding her hand while she walks toward the cliff.**[7]
>
> —Dee Brestin

"Write" Before You Speak the Truth

In the book of Matthew (7:1–5) we are warned to take a good look at ourselves before we try to help our brother (friend). Here is an exercise to do prior to speaking the truth to your friend:

1. Take out a fresh piece of paper and write out (longhand) Matthew 7:1–5 and Proverbs 3:5.

2. Write out as honest a confession as you can, telling the Lord ALL the reasons you feel you need to talk to your friend, ALL your feelings, and anything else that comes to mind.

3. Write a prayer asking the Lord for *His* knowledge and *His* understanding (and ask Him to help you differentiate between leaning on your own understanding and seeing His understanding). Ask the Spirit to examine your heart and to see if there is anything in you that needs to be cleansed, forgiven, or changed.

4. If you still feel the urging to go to the person, then prayerfully ask the Lord to go with you and guide your words and your attitude as you speak and to prepare the heart of your friend to have the ears to hear what you are saying.

> **In your anger do not sin.**
>
> (Ephesians 4:26)

> **When a relationship is strained, I like to address it in writing. This allows me to sit with it for a few days, pray about it, seek wise counsel regarding it, and most of all, it keeps me from lashing out in anger.**
>
> —Marita Littauer, coauthor of *Wired That Way*

Asking for and Being Open to Input

> **As iron sharpens iron, so a friend sharpens a friend.**
>
> (Proverbs 27:17 NLT)

> **Perfume and incense bring joy to the heart, and the pleasantness of one's friend springs from his earnest counsel.**
>
> (Proverbs 27:9)

I have blind spots, don't you? I don't always know how I come across. I can mean one thing but be understood a completely different way. I need safe friends who love the Lord, love me, and help me see the parts of me that I don't see very well. I need friends to love me in the places that aren't so lovely. This, in turn, helps my roots go down deeper into the soil of God's love and truth and causes me to grow.

The truth my friends have given me in love has really helped me in my marriage. When Russ and I aren't connecting or we've had a fight, my friends have not only been a safe haven for me to cry and vent, they have also been willing to give me the truth in love. They have gently and clearly helped me see what I contributed to the argument or revealed to me a destructive pattern of behavior or an unrealistic expectation I have of my husband that is exasperating him and leaving me depressed. At times it's hard to see truth, but being open to input and even asking for input is truly invaluable in growing friendships.

One of the blessings available to you in a healthy, growing friendship is the opportunity to be sharpened by one another. How well do you do when a friend holds up a mirror and shows you some areas that could use some help and healing? Take note that this input is more easily assimilated if the friend that is extending it has a heart full of love and grace for you as well as truth. Listen to how Nancy H. describes the love and truth she received from her friend Katie:

> My friend Katie would just call me or ride her bike over (we lived near each other) and hang out with me and eat egg salad sandwiches and talk about God. She would say stuff like "When are you going to start saying no to hanging out with the Buddhist?" "When are you going to start trusting God and tithing?" It was basically a huge control issue for me with God, to be obedient when He said in His Word not to do something, or to start doing something He asked me to do, like pray for my enemies. God would give me a word (like James 4 when I would be praying about fighting with my ex-husband, or trusting God with little bits of my issues), and so I began to trust Him more and more. My life is 100 percent different now, and I owe it all to God and the way He worked through Katie. She showed me what a REAL friend does. . . . She supported me, challenged me, and loved me through it all. We had quite a few conflicts. It was not easy. But we are TRUE friends in that we are truthful with each other. We are not surface friends.

Isn't it awesome that our Lord places people in our lives to help us grow in grace and in truth?

Lessons From "The Greats"

Communicate, swallow your pride, and pick your battles.

Light Touch

> The most wasted of all days is that during which one has not laughed.[8]
>
> —Nicolas De Chamfort

Life's Too Short to Take Yourself So Seriously

He who covers over an offense promotes love.

(Proverbs 17:9)

A few months ago our church held a women's bowling night. Now, I am not much of a bowler, but I am all about hanging out with girlfriends, eating pizza, and laughing. I was not disappointed that night!

I was paired up with my friend Nancy and soon found out that she was only planning on staying for a little while because she had higher priorities for the evening: watching the season premiere of her favorite TV show. I, along with a few other gals, playfully harassed Nancy about her obviously misplaced priorities, but she is getting so healthy in her identity in Christ that she couldn't care less what we thought and was happily looking forward to both parts of her evening.

Sure enough, as eight o'clock approached Nancy bid us farewell and headed out the door, and we continued on with our evening of knocking down random pins and eating greasy pizza. At about eight-fifteen my cell phone rang. It was Nancy. She said, "Do you want to laugh?" "Of course," I responded. Nancy continued, "I was driving down the freeway looking forward to watching my show when I thought to myself, *Hmm . . . my feet feel a little weird.* I looked down and realized that in my excitement to get to my television, I forgot to take off my bowling shoes!" I screamed with laughter, covered the phone, and let the rest of the ladies at the alley know what was going on. I could hear Nancy laughing as I shared her news. It got even funnier after that because Nancy let me know that she wasn't turning the car around to come back because she didn't want to miss any of her show. Instead, when she got to her house where a few other families had gathered to watch the show, she proudly modeled her new style: shoes with the word *rental* written on the side in big black marker.

Now, I want to be clear, Nancy is not some ditzy airhead that goes around making a fool of herself. She is an intelligent, thoughtful woman who has learned (by the grace of God) not to take herself so seriously. (She is also a very honest woman and returned her bowling shoes the very next day along with a detailed explanation of how she came to take them home with her. The teen working the counter that day didn't seem that interested or amused.)

When you make a mistake you have the option of beating yourself up or throwing your hands up, laughing at yourself, and reminding yourself that this is an opportunity to grow in humility and to remember that God "gives grace to the humble" (Proverbs 3:34).

The other great thing about not taking yourself so seriously and growing in humility is that you are more likely to be able to extend grace to others, shrug off their mistakes, and not be so easily offended.

Have Fun With Each Other

If I need to laugh I have learned to call my *paisans*. Paisan is Italian slang for "friend," and it is the name my friends Sheri and Shirley have dubbed our threesome even though only one of us is a true Italian. Shirley is Italian, Sheri is married to an Italian, and I'm just Italian by association. (I've had people ask me all my life if I'm Italian—it might be the distinctive laugh, the tendency I have to get all choked up over the littlest sentimentality, or my inability to tell a story without a lot of hand gestures.) Whenever the three of us get together it's not long before we are laughing LOUDLY. It doesn't seem to matter where we go. The last time we got together we went to a discount store (Marshall's) and spent three hours (yes, I said three) going up and down the aisles and laughing. We got a few interesting looks, but for the most part we got comments like "We want to hang out with you guys!" and "It's a party wherever you go!" About ten minutes into our shopping adventure I realized that I had my camera in my purse, and that got us started taking pictures of one another holding giant teapots and random ceramic animals with feathered wreaths sitting jauntily atop our heads. We even had the checkout lady take a picture of us at the end of our time together. (She didn't look amused, but you could tell she needed a little more joy infused into her life.)

Laughing is good for the soul and it's good for your health. Not only do we release endorphins when we laugh, I recently heard Women of Faith speaker Marilyn Meberg say that "it even gives your internal organs a workout!" Make sure that you take the time to laugh with your friends. If you have a personality that is a little more on the serious side, intentionally spend time with friends who can loosen you up a bit.

I have a picture of Sheri that I keep right over my desk. It is a classic shot that reminds me to laugh and to hold my friends with a light touch. I captured this moment on film as the paisans drove to one of our inexpensive but priceless adventures. Sheri's head is sticking out the sunroof of Shirley's car, and her mouth is wide open as she screams with glee over the fact that it's a girls' day out. Under the picture is a card that reads, "Laugh so hard that you go into silent laugh mode and you come dangerously close to falling out of your chair, but you don't."[9] Isn't that a great goal in friendship and in life? The Bible puts it this way: "A happy heart makes the face cheerful. . . . The cheerful heart has a continual feast" (Proverbs 15:13, 15).

 ## Ponder

When was the last time someone spoke the truth to you in love? Was it difficult to hear at the time? How did you react?

Has there been a time when you were wounded by someone who was trying to hurt you with the truth?

When was the last time you extended grace? Received grace?

Do you think you are more naturally a grace person or a truth person?

Did you find yourself stuck anywhere in this chapter? Did you find a place that needs the healing touch of God or the strength and courage to move forward?

Pray

The only thing that counts is faith expressing itself through love.

(Galatians 5:6)

Lord, I need your help to do the loving thing in my friendships. I confess that oftentimes I can get caught up in who is right and who is wrong, or who is good and who is bad, when you are calling me to look at the real question, "What is the loving thing to do?" Show me when it is grace that you want me to extend and show me when it is truth. Help me work out differences with a heart that is humble and honest. Help me take responsibility when I have wounded another with my attitude, words, or actions. Help me to extend forgiveness to my friends, keeping in mind all that you have forgiven me for. Most of all, Lord, help me to enjoy my friends, and tenderly and gently hold our friendship as the precious gift it is from you. In Jesus' name, amen.

Apply

Laughing and Living With the Daisies in Your Chain

Rent a classic movie and have an impromptu girls' night or just show up at your girlfriend's house when you know her husband is going to be out of town on a business trip. Bring a movie for the two of you and a movie for the kids to watch in the other room. (Some of my favorites include: *While You Were Sleeping, Sabrina, Return to Me,* and *Ever After.*)

Leave your friend a message that only she will "get" (voice mail or e-mail).

Keep your camera close at hand so you can capture those funny moments. (You never know when you might find yourself doubled over in laughter.)

Send your friend a funny card, or better yet make a card with a picture you've taken when the two of you were laughing your heads off.

Letters From a Friend

Dear Friend,

I wanted to share with you the ways in which you have touched my life with the beauty that comes from within you.

I appreciate your gift of listening and how you truly care about me and my family. Thank you also for being a woman of grace and of truth. I appreciate that you speak the truth with me, that I don't have to guess what you think or how you feel. This is very valuable to me.

Although I know you deal with struggles and weaknesses as I do, I want you to know that I have seen you learn to be at rest with yourself more and more. This has invited me to do the same thing. Your heart for God is so beautiful to see and has inspired me in my own relationship with Him.

God continues to bless me through the women in my life, and you are among these. I think it a privilege to walk this journey with you, my dear friend. God has truly loved me through your touch, your words, and your warm and loving home with many cups of tea.

I love you, my friend, and I pray that God continues to use you in mighty ways. . . . Many blessings to you as you continue on the path of your loving heavenly Father.

Love you,
Nancy

Chapter 6

Forming the Crown

Once you have a chain of daisies, loop the flowers into a circle, make a slightly larger slit in the last stem, and fit the entire head of the first flower through it.

Rejoice with those who rejoice; mourn with those who mourn.

(Romans 12:15)

The pain was steady, choking off the air in my throat and causing my head to pound. I gripped the steering wheel a little tighter and tried to breathe. I became very aware, very quickly, that I needed someone to help me. I called my friend Nancy as the tears streamed down my face on the drive home from my grandma's nursing home. I called her because I knew I needed someone to pray for me that very minute. I needed someone to ask Jesus to give me the strength to get through this time.

My grandma is dying. Just writing that causes a new wave of grief to wash over me. Not that it's a new thought. My grandma has been struggling for a while and has been in the nursing home for over a year. As of late, I have even been praying that God would have mercy on her and take her home soon. Ever since my grandpa died eight years ago it seems that she has been anxious to leave. So on this day I thought I was doing okay, but Grandma recently had a stroke, and now she's in hospice care, and today she wouldn't open her eyes when she talked to me.

Nancy listened to my sobs as I drove down the road, and then she quietly began to pray for me. The pain began to dissipate; I welcomed the air back into my lungs and the clarity to my head. I became aware once again through the presence and prayers of my friend who was coming alongside me that I would get through this and that I am not alone.

In Galatians 6:2 (NASB) the apostle Paul exhorts us to "bear one another's burdens, and thereby fulfill the law of Christ" and in Romans 12:15 we are taught to "rejoice with those who rejoice; mourn with those who mourn."

In order to have a friendship that flourishes, a deep connected relationship, it is important to live life together. In order to turn a chain of flowers and of friends into the beauty of a crown you must loop that chain into a circle, causing the flowers to come alongside one another. We accomplish this by joining our friends in the simplicities of life.

Simplicities

**Then those who feared the Lord talked with each other,
and the Lord listened and heard.**

(Malachi 3:16)

How much of life could be made more enjoyable by doing the simple things together?

My neighbor Michele and I often joined one another in the simplest things in life. We traded baby-sitting so we could get hair, doctor, and dentist appointments in. We picked stuff up at the store for one another. We sat together in our pajamas and drank tea while the kids watched *Barney* and *Blue's Clues*. But perhaps one of my favorite ways that we enjoyed the simplicity of life together was by cooking for one another, more specifically by trading dinner nights. We each picked one night of the week, and on that night we would double our dinner recipe and then bring dinner over to one another. This gave us each a night off from cooking, gave the kids a variety of menus (my daughter LOVED whatever Michele made—especially if it was with Hamburger Helper), and communicated love to each other through this simple act. It was a way for us to come alongside one another. As a matter of fact, this practice had such an impact on our lives that when Michele's family told us they were moving, my six-year-old's first response as she collapsed into my arms was "Who's going to make dinner for us on Thursdays?"

Here are some ways to come alongside our friends:

- Wrap Christmas gifts or label and stamp your Christmas cards together.
- Work out together or go walking regularly together.
- Rearrange furniture, redecorate, or re-accessorize one another's homes.
- Call each other spontaneously and meet at the park or a fast-food playland with the kids.
- Make dinner together (check out *www.dreamdinners.com*).
- Carve pumpkins, search for Easter eggs, bake heart-shaped Valentine cookies together, have Thanksgiving Day breakfast together and watch the parade on television, go to Fourth of July parades and fireworks shows together.
- Do errands together on your lunch hour.
- Study for a class together.

My girlfriend Tiffany is married to a Navy Seal, and when I told her that I was writing a book about friendship, this tough-as-nails gal immediately broke down into tears. She told me about the special time she had living on the Navy base with the other wives. She told me these wives formed a tight bond just by doing life together while their husbands were away for months at a time. The friendships she formed with women who were going through the same thing she was became a way that God came alongside her and let her know that she was not alone. Live life with your girlfriends by coming alongside them.

Often we call each other or meet for a meal, coffee, or go for a walk. Sometimes we have to resort to sleepovers. My friend Leslie just came over with her dog Bruno and we watched a movie . . . fun and inexpensive.

—Nancy H.

Sorrows

Many might have failed beneath the bitterness of their trial had they not found a friend.[1]

—Charles H. Spurgeon

The little girls formed a tight circle in the church vestibule. As I got closer I noticed eyes that were wet with tears and shoulders that rose and fell as they quietly cried together. I felt grateful that these young cousins had one another at this their great-grandmother's funeral, for there is comfort to be had in a circle of friends. Sorrow is somehow easier to bear when it is carried on the shoulders of many.

Here are some ways to come alongside in times of sorrow:

- Sit *quietly* with your friend, remembering that you don't have to fix it, you just need to care.
- Drive her wherever she needs to go.
- Make phone calls for her.
- Clean her house.
- Rally families and organize a meal schedule or fill her freezer with easy-to-reheat dinners.
- Pray for her.
- Take her children to the park or have them over for the night so she can have some space.
- Bring her and her family snacks/meals to the hospital.
- Send cards.

My friend Kathy writes about the power of love released through the simple act of sending a note in times of sorrow:

> One of the best ways friends have been loving to me, helped fill my cup, was by writing me notes of encouragement, sending me cards, and giving me words they had read that caused them to think of me. . . . *The majority of the time,* what was most encouraging or helpful for me was just that a friend wrote something for ME. She was thinking of ME. I highly recommend that

**whenever you feel a yearning to write something to a
friend, do everything you can to just do it. Don't beat
yourself up if you don't get to it, but even if you do it
once in your lifetime, it will touch an empty void in your
friend that she may not have even known existed.**

Handle With Care

Be careful during times of sorrow if you feel a compulsive desire
to:

Cheer up your friend. In Proverbs we are warned, "Like one who
takes away a garment on a cold day, or like vinegar poured on soda,
is one who sings songs to a heavy heart" (25:20).

Remind her of her blessings. I'm sure you've heard well-meaning
people say at a funeral, "Well, she's in a better place," or "Just be
grateful that you had as many good years with her as you did." While
these thoughts may indeed be true, they can also deny the pain the
individual is feeling (or even worse, make them feel bad about the
feelings of sadness they are having) and interfere in their personal
grieving process.

The bottom line? Listen to and observe your friend and prayerfully
let her take the lead. If you still feel the desire to cheer her up, perhaps you need to work through some of what *you* are feeling during
this time of sorrow. Pray about this and seek wise counsel through
another friend, pastor, or counselor.

Joys

**Wreaths or crowns were worn at joyous occasions,
such as weddings or feasts.[2]**

Jesus also lives in the celebratory times, or as my writer friends
Shirley and Sheri and I call it, the "jumping and screaming" times.
Whether it is a promotion, an anniversary, the birth of a grandchild,
the engagement of a daughter, or the call about the first book con-

tract, Jesus often shows up in the shouts of a girlfriend or a group of girlfriends. One of my favorite moments of joy came during the birth of my daughter. I will let my friend Sue tell you about it in a letter she wrote to my little girl on her "birthday."

The Day "Grace" Was Born

On the day you were born, the sun shone bright in a cloudless sky as if to say your way into our lives was clear. . . .

On the day you were born, your mommy's dearest friends paced and prayed, awaiting word of your arrival.

All told, we were six anxious women who dearly love your mommy—five of six with strong feelings you would be a girl.

When the news finally came that "Grace" was born, we squealed and cried tears of utter joy. You were placed by God in the center of a circle of women who will love and nurture you in things both feminine and spiritual. . . .

On the day you were born, your daddy was by your side when we first glimpsed your dark little head and beautiful pink body.

He touched your hands and feet ever so gently and whispered words of comfort and welcome—his lips so near your face.

Perchance he sensed at first the joy you would bring him or thought of the honor it would be one day to walk you down the aisle. . . .

As one who witnessed your first hour of life, I wanted to let it forever be known to you, little Gracie . . .

You had my prayers before you first breathed and my devotion e'er after.

Of course, the day my daughter was born was one of our family's most wonderful, celebratory days, and having friends and family around us really multiplied that joy. When I think back to that day, to my girlfriends standing in the hallway pacing back and forth with joyful expectation, I can't help but beam. My little girl always asks me to tell her the funny part of the story of the day she was born, which was when my girlfriends found out that the baby was "Grace" (as opposed to "Jeremy" if it had been a boy). They screamed *so* loudly that nurses went running into the hallway to find out what the emergency was. That memory makes me giggle and makes my daughter shine. Yes, having friends to come alongside you in times of joy is a true gift, and the memories remain long after the day ends.

I also remember a day not so long ago when the galleys of my first book showed up on my front porch. I had no idea what a galley was since I'd never written a book before, so the minute I opened the thick manila envelope, I started jumping up and down because all the pages of the book were there, laid out in color just the way they would appear in a few months when the book would release to the stores. I called my friend Andrea, who was driving to some appointment. She immediately turned her car toward my house. She and my friend Heather were on my doorstep within minutes. I got the camera out and took a picture of Andrea and Heather turning the pages of that book, looking as if *they* had just given birth. It was awesome . . . another moment of joy that was made even more memorable because of the friends who stood beside me celebrating as if it were their celebration too. And indeed it was because I know that without the prayers, support, and encouragement of my daisies, I would not be able to do what I do.

Here are some examples of times to jump and scream with your friend(s):

- Promotions or new jobs
- Graduations
- Milestones
- Birthdays
- Anniversaries
- Weddings
- Confirmations, baby dedications, baptisms
- Children's/grandchildren's milestones
- New homes
- Answered prayers

Creative ways to jump and scream:

- Bring her a balloon bouquet or flowers.
- Take her out to dinner or dessert.
- Leave a loud message on her voice mail.
- Treat her to a pedicure.
- Throw a party.
- Purchase a little keepsake so she can remember this day.
- Make a banner with your kids and tape it to her garage door.

Letting Them Know

In order for your friends to come alongside you, they need to know when you have moments to celebrate. Don't you hate finding out that you missed a friend's birthday or special event because you didn't know about it? Their big day snuck by because they didn't tell you it was a big day. When that happens, I feel disappointed that I didn't get to celebrate them or celebrate with them. Let your friends know about your jumping and screaming moments. They WANT to celebrate . . . it brings them joy to celebrate with you . . . to share in and rejoice in what God is doing in your life or just in the simple fact that you were born! I just got an e-mail yesterday that brought tears to my eyes. It is a perfect example of "letting them know" she had reason to celebrate. . . .

> **Dear Friends,**
> I just wanted to share one of my greatest moments with some of you. As you know, all I ever talk about is my kids, and it is usually about "the struggle," not the accomplishments. So today I wanted to share one of my greatest accomplishments: My daughter Alyssa graduated early from high school today. I could not be prouder of the person she is and I just wanted to share that with you!!!
> **Jayne**

Hiding Your Joy

Rejoice in the Lord always. I will say it again: Rejoice! Let your gentleness be evident to all. The Lord is near.

(Philippians 4:4–5)

I grew up feeling like I needed to hide my moments of celebration or play them down. I felt that if I got a good thing, it meant someone else wouldn't get anything or that my good thing would trigger jealousy in someone else and cause them to hate me and/or abandon me. So I learned not to make a big deal out of my triumphs and victories (which were really God's triumphs and victories). I entered adulthood living with this scarcity mentality, believing that there's only so much to go around. Through the study of the truth of God's Word, prayer, friendship, and sitting under the teaching of those wiser than me, I have learned (and continue to learn) that we serve a God of abundance "who is able to do immeasurably more than all we ask or imagine" (Ephesians 3:20). God is no respecter of persons, and just because He blesses one person doesn't mean that He won't bless another. It's not like He has only so many cookies and if He gives one to someone, someone else won't get any. God created the universe and everything in it!

As my eyes were opened to the lie I'd been believing, I felt freer to enjoy the blessings I'd been given. As a matter of fact, my very first year in God's Word resonated with this theme, and as a result the first talk I ever gave was entitled "Seize the Day" and was based on 1 Timothy 6:17 (NKJV): "The living God, who gives us richly all things to enjoy."

Do not hide your blessings. Do not keep your joy to yourself for fear of making someone else feel bad. You do not have that power. Instead, rejoice in the blessings, praise God for the answered prayers, and allow your friends and family the privilege of coming alongside you and celebrating; in doing so they will surely be inspired to wait in joyful expectation for their El Shaddai (the All-Sufficient One) to do great and mighty works in their own lives.

Not Enjoying Her Joy

Have there been times of joy and celebration in your friend's life that have triggered negative feelings in your own as you waited for God to answer your prayer(s)?

- Your friend moves into a larger home while you are still in an apartment.
- Your friend gets pregnant while you struggle with infertility.
- Your friend gets a promotion while you are still looking for a job.
- Your friend's marriage is thriving while yours is going through a season of suffering.
- Your friend is able to stay home with her kids while you need to work to help make ends meet.

I encourage you to bring these feelings to your heavenly Father, who already knows they are there. "If the Spirit of God detects anything wrong, He does not ask you to put it right; He asks you to accept the light, and He will put it right."[3]

I have been a witness to times when a friend has confessed her feelings: "I really want to be happy for you, but I have to admit this reminds me of what's missing in my own life." (These were usually shared at a later date, not during the actual moment of celebration.) And I must tell you that most of the time those feelings were met with love and compassion. So if you can tell your friend senses that you have these feelings, or if she asks you, or if you feel you want to talk them through with her at a future date (not too close to the day of celebration so as to take away from the joy your friend is feeling), it certainly can be an opportunity for growth in you and your friendship. This is not to say that every time we feel a swelling of discontent, envy, or jealousy we blurt it out of our mouths, but when after you pray it seems like the right choice, go ahead and work it out with her and ask her to pray for you as well that God would continue to help you celebrate the blessings in the lives of those around you.

> **To be able to find joy in another's joy,**
> **that is the secret of happiness.**[4]
>
> —George Bernanos

Crisis

> **The support of my friends was crucial to my recovery.**
> **I honestly wonder if I would be here today without the**
> **love, care, and encouragement of my friends during**
> **the bone marrow transplant. Some friends helped with**
> **cleaning, cooking, and errands. Others prayed with me**
> **or took my son Kyle to the movies. When I got stronger**
> **they took me out to lunch, and Kyle and I joined them on**
> **a day trip to somewhere fun.**
>
> —Georgia Shaffer, producer of *The Mourning Glory Minute*

As I researched for this book I read through many old journals and found myself laughing and crying at the memories. I also found myself amazed at how the Lord showed up in my life through the presence of friends. Here is an example of one of those times of crisis that I recorded in the pages of my journal. Within a three-week period in the joyful month of January 2000:

- The fire trucks showed up when I almost single-handedly burned the house down by forgetting about the chicken I'd put on to boil (because I was busy talking on the phone while I did it) and taking a leisurely shopping trip through Costco.

- We had to live with the disgusting aroma of burnt chicken for a week before we moved out to have the air ducts, walls, and furniture professionally cleaned.

- I endured the most stressful work situation in my life, which ultimately ended with my decision to resign.

- My grandpa landed in the hospital for an angioplasty.

- I found a lump.

- Russ and I weren't exactly connecting.

- To top it all off, my eighteen-month-old daughter got a double ear infection, and I spent two hours at the pediatrician (which included holding Grace's feverish little body down for a breathing treatment while she screamed).

When I finally got Grace into her car seat, I discovered that my car was only interested in driving in reverse for about three feet before stalling in a precarious half-in half-out position in the parking lot. I proceeded to panic and thought I was locked in my car. (The electricity shut down and I couldn't get the door open.) After calling AAA, I dialed my friend Sue's number. When I heard her voice I broke down in tears and all I could utter was a weird, strangled cat sound, to which Sue responded, "Tracy, is that you?" I only had time enough to tell her "I dropped my basket" before the eighteen-year-old surfer dude AAA worker was knocking on my window. By the time I got home twenty minutes later, my daughter was fast asleep in her car seat and two of my friends were waiting on my porch. They brought the necessities for times such as these . . . French fries, Diet Coke, and flowers. Attached to the flowers was a card that read:

**A-tisket, a-tasket, I'm here to hold
your basket . . . anytime.**

I later found out that Sue had called Andrea as soon as she got off the phone with me and simply said, "Tracy dropped her basket." That was enough information to alert my friend that crisis had occurred and "presence" was needed. Sue and Andrea willingly dropped whatever plans they had and came rushing to my side. Their action in my little crisis communicated louder than words that I was not alone and that God would help me when I needed it.

While it is definitely not the most godly book or model of Christian living, the novel *Divine Secrets of the Ya-Ya Sisterhood*[5] had one phrase that perfectly described a common occurrence in the life of a woman. One girlfriend would say, "I dropped my basket" to communicate to another girlfriend that she had pretty much lost it. Our circle of friends adopted the phrase and used it when we needed one another. I think it is particularly appropriate because it reminds me of what I *am* able to do for my friend and what I am *not* able to do for her.

Oftentimes when I am with a friend who is experiencing a time of great sorrow or crisis, I feel a deep desire to fix it. I have such a hard time seeing my friend in pain that I want to do whatever I can to take that pain away from her. I am learning more and more every day that this is not a power that I possess. I am not God, and I do not have the ability to . . .

- Make her husband come back
- Keep the accident from happening
- Deliver her from her addiction
- Heal her from her cancer
- Bring her runaway home

I cannot save my friend, but I know the One who can. What I *can* do is come alongside my friend and in so doing help her hold her basket. It is as I come alongside that I make myself available to be a vessel that God can use in the ways He who is all-wise chooses to.

Drawing Near

In times of crisis, in times when you or your friend's basket is on the ground, it is important to remember that action speaks louder than words. It is time to rally the troops and show up. That isn't to say that you can always be there, but as much as is possible, attempt to help.

There might be times when you ask your friend if there is anything you can do, and she says something like "Not that I can think of." While it is vitally important to respect a person's boundaries—especially if they are clear that they need some space—I recommend taking part in a fivefold action plan (which can be done in minutes) for times of crisis.

1. Pray for discernment. When there is a serious crisis occurring, it is often challenging for a person to think clearly and then communicate what they need.

2. Think through your friend's personality, your relationship, and what you know about her. (Does she usually like having people around, or does she prefer small groups and lots of downtime?)

3. Ask yourself what would be helpful for you if the roles were reversed. What would you want your friends to do for you?

4. Ask the Lord to tell you what to do and then give you the strength and boldness to do it.

5. Ask the Lord to guard your heart and help you extend grace. Sometimes we can get our feelings hurt when we are only trying to help. Keep in mind that the friend you are trying to help is in a crisis and she needs extra space and extra grace. If she gets mad and lashes out, in all likelihood it is not *all* about you but about the circumstances she's dealing with.

If you are ever confused or at a total loss as to how to best support someone, simply ask them what would be most helpful. If they aren't able to give you a clear answer, ask if there was ever a time recently when they felt a bit better. If so, what were they doing? This question may trigger a suggestion. If they state they need to be alone for a while, don't take it personally. That may be exactly what they require.

—Georgia Shaffer, producer of *The Mourning Glory Minute*

Ways to Come Alongside in Times of Crisis

- Go to the scene of the crisis and be available (hospital, home, place of work).

- Keep your eyes peeled and your ears open to ways you can help. (For example, if you overhear a person say they just don't know how they're going to make all those calls, ask if they'd like you to do it.)
- Respond to requests for help, and if you can't help, try to find someone who can stay in contact and let you know how you can help later.
- PRAY for the individual and all those who surround them.

A Warning

A small disclaimer for the friend whose life seems to involve one crisis after another: In these cases I advise you to pray for wisdom and discernment. Ask the Lord to guide you, because sometimes the most loving thing for you to do is to communicate the truth in love. Let your friend know that you have observed that she seems to be comfortable living in crisis mode. It may also be important to ask the Lord to show you if there is anything in you that needs to change. For example, do *you* ever ask for help from this friend or any friend when you are in crisis? Are you always the helper (enabler) and never the one who needs (or lets others know that you need) help? You might be contributing to the problem, and God may want to deliver you from this pattern of behavior.

Friends come alongside one another. Friends do life together. Friends show up and in so doing communicate with action the profound spiritual truth that *we are not alone*.

My friend Nancy and I have been through life, death, and everything in between. She was at my side (as the labor and delivery nurse!) for the births of both my children; we've been establishing a church together in partnership with our husbands, who are both pastors; she attended my grandpa's funeral; and I spoke on her behalf at her mother's funeral. We have laughed uproariously at silly movies and gone on crazy vacations. We've celebrated milestones and battled through times of spiritual warfare. Friends live life side by side, and this is what happens to a chain of daisies when you take the time to loop them into the shape of a crown.

Ponder

What are some of your favorite things/activities that you do with your friends?

What was one of the most joyous times in your life?

What was one of the most difficult times in your life?

Did your friends know about these seasons?

How did they come alongside you during these seasons?

What did it mean to you to have them standing next to you while you went through this joy or sorrow?

Does coming alongside a friend come naturally, or do you have to be more intentional about it? Why do you think this is?

Did you find yourself stuck anywhere in this chapter? Did you find a place that needs the healing touch of God or the strength and courage to move forward?

Pray

A friend loves at all times.

(Proverbs 17:17)

Father God, help me to be the kind of friend who "loves at all times." Open my eyes to the opportunities to come alongside my friends and help me know what to do once I get there. Guide my words and actions. Lord, I want to receive the blessing of a friend who will come alongside me as well. Please bring women into my life who will do so and please open my heart to allow the women who are already in my life to do so. Help me not only to invite their presence into my joys, sorrows, simplicities, and crises, but to welcome it when they arrive. I confess that this is hard because I feel _____ (confess any feelings here) *but I know that I am not meant to travel through this life alone. So I choose to receive the gift of companionship and help that you offer me through your people. In Jesus' name, amen.*

 ## Apply

Coming Alongside the Daisies in Your Chain

Show up! Attend the next major and minor events in your friend's life—even if she says "It's no big deal."

The next time God answers a prayer in your life or blesses you unexpectedly, call your friends and let them know. . . . This will give you an opportunity to "jump and scream" and praise God together.

Letters From a Friend

Dear Friends and Family,

I love you and I want you to know that I couldn't have made it through this year without you.

Throughout this battle with cancer I have had a sense that "God is with me." But it hasn't just been my faith that has gotten me through; it's been your faith as well. Your prayers and support have meant the world to me. You cried with me when I needed to cry. You laughed with me when I needed to laugh. You have stood beside me this entire time, and I want you to know how much I appreciate you.

Thank you for . . .

Showing up at my house the minute I found out that I had a tumor

Going with me to doctors' appointments (including the one where they told me I had cancer and had only six months to a year)

Not taking "no hope" as the final answer and finding me a doctor who would operate

Taking care of my four children . . . getting them to and from school, to and from practices, all the while making sure they had clean clothes to wear and a hug to take with them

Cooking meals for my family for months on end

Bringing me grilled cheese sandwiches when that's all I could stomach

Writing me notes, cards, and letters to encourage me and to let me know you were praying for me and Lou and the kids

Sending thoughtful gifts that reminded me of your love in tangible ways

Taking me away for the weekend. . . . I loved our girls' trip in Mammoth, laughing and skiing and hanging out in the Jacuzzi. Thank you for encouraging me to go even though I was uncertain at first

Lending me a pretty dress for the gala . . . it helped me look beautiful when I felt anything but

Showing up day after day when I spent a month in the hospital after the second surgery

Forcing me to get in my wheelchair and get out in the sunshine instead of staying cooped up in my room

Driving me wherever I needed to go and walking with me even when I was slow

This list only begins to cover the many ways that you have come alongside me this past year. The bottom line is this: Of course I needed God, but I also needed you. You are each an answer to prayer and a blessing in my life that I won't soon forget. I love you all.

Love,

Julie Anne Luepke

January 9, 1964 – May 16, 2007

Note: After quietly observing Julie's inner circle come alongside her, I approached her to see if she would like to write a letter (as a surprise for her friends and family) to include in this book. She was ecstatic and looked forward to the opportunity to express her gratitude in black and white. Six weeks after the completion of the letter, Julie went home to be with Jesus. Her "life song" lingers on.

Chapter 7

Wearing the Crown

Wearing the crown is celebrating who I am and celebrating who my friends are, because we are all made in the image of Him who is beauty and love!

A crown of flowers is more demonstrative of the nature of God than a single flower.

A faithful friend is an image of God.[1]

—French Proverb

For as the earth bursts with spring wildflowers, and as a garden cascades with blossoms, so the Master, God, brings righteousness into full bloom and puts praise on display before the nations.

(Isaiah 61:11 THE MESSAGE)

In my circle of friends I am known as the idea girl ("Why don't we . . ."), the cheerleader ("We can do it!"), and the impromptu/impulsive jumper-inner who drags as many with her as possible. So when I showed up at one of our girlfriend gatherings and gushed enthusiastically, "I have a great idea; it's something we can all do together!" I was met with a few smirks, giggles, and possibly even an under-the-breath "Here we go again . . ." These responses did not faze me, and I proceeded to tell my friends that I'd heard about this amazing event called the Avon 3-Day. It involves walking sixty miles over the course of three days to raise money for breast cancer research. I told the girls that I thought we should be a team, train together, and raise ten thousand dollars together.

I was prepared for the responses . . .

"Sixty miles . . . wow, Tracy, that's far!"

"We have a whole year; we can work up to it. I'm an aerobics instructor. I can help you guys train for it!"

"Ten thousand dollars is a lot of money to raise!"

"We have to dream big! It's a great cause! I just know people will rally!"

"I don't know . . ."

"Come on, it will be FUN!"

That night *one* of my friends agreed to do the walk with me, and after a few days of gushing enthusiastically, we had convinced two other girlfriends: one to walk with us and the other to be our team captain.

We launched into a steady stream of walking, talking, and writing letters. We even made a short movie to help others catch the vision of what we were trying to do in the hope that they would help us reach our ten-thousand-dollar goal. It was a great year of training, preparation, and bonding.

The big day arrived. It was a foggy autumn morning. After an inspirational send-off, we started out on our first twenty-plus-mile day. I was on fire for about the first two hours, and then my feet started to hurt. Four hours later, when we got to our lunch pit stop, my upbeat, cheerleader, "We can do it" attitude had disintegrated and was replaced by a sarcastic "I don't wanna," "This isn't fun," "What was I thinking?" and "Are you seriously telling me I have to get up and do this again tomorrow?" attitude.

The good news is that my compadres found my attitude highly amusing—a side of me, in fact, that they had never seen before. (Up until this point only my husband had been graced with this much authenticity from me.) Other than entertainment value, my rapid decline into negativity did have an unexpected blessing . . . it illuminated the gifts that I so appreciate in my friends. You see, while my personality may have been the one that got us going, my girlfriends' personalities and gifts were what kept us moving forward.

My friend Andrea has a strong, no-nonsense personality. She is also a forward thinker, and when she found out that on the Avon 3-Day you sleep in tents at night (which you set up yourself after having walked twenty miles), she made other arrangements for us.

(Her parents picked us up the first night, and we took a taxi to a hotel the second night.) I initially told Andrea that if we didn't sleep in the tents we would miss out on the whole experience of the 3-Day, but she went ahead and made the arrangements anyway. Andrea is not one to be easily dissuaded or to bow down to people pleasing . . . a blessing indeed, because by the end of the first day of walking I told her how glad I was that she didn't listen to me. However, I think I said it more like "I am so NOT sleeping in a tent tonight!" with very little gratitude in my voice. She took that as the thank-you that it was intended to be.

My friend Michele has a power-it-out and make-it-beautiful personality. While she was probably the most concerned about the physicality of the walk when we first started training, she was the one who put her bedazzled head down and walked FAST and steady. Michele wore a different color-coordinated, bedazzled do-rag on her head each day and kept our spirits up by talking about the best skin care products on the market and what color she was going to paint her kitchen next.

My friend Persa, our team captain, has the nurturing and by-all-means-never-let-them-starve Greek personality. She got us registered on the day of the event, she brought snacks for us, she drove us to the starting line, and she called our husbands and made sure they knew the details of where we were each step of the way. She also gave us daily care packages complete with notes and prayers of encouragement and new pajamas to change into (after our tired-out bodies could no longer stand the feeling of sweaty lycra pressed against them). Persa was also the friend who brought balloons, cameras, and signs for us when we finally crossed the finish line.

We finished that 3-Day journey triumphantly because we came together with our different personalities and different gifts and talents and we *moved out*. We celebrated and embraced our differences and in so doing we not only enjoyed life, we showed the world a more complete view of Christ.

Friendship exhibits a glorious "nearness by resemblance" to Heaven itself where the very multitude of the blessed (which no man can number) increases the fruition which each has of God. For every soul, seeing Him in her own way, doubtless communicates that unique vision to all the rest.[2]

—C. S. Lewis

In Scripture we are taught that we are each created in the "image of God" (Genesis 1:27). We are all image bearers. When we wear our crown of friendship and celebrate the gifts we uniquely possess and that our friends uniquely possess, we glorify God and give the world a more complete view of who He is.

However, more often than not, instead of celebrating our unique differences, women compare themselves to one another . . . and not in a good way.

"I wish I was more outgoing like Mary or more organized like Lisa."

"If only I could sing like Tina or look like Janet."

"Why can't I be more content in life like Sarah or more motivated like Angie?"

When We Compare, We Miss What's There

In comparing ourselves to others we often miss what God has placed in us. We miss the unique qualities, gifts, and personality traits that He has placed in us and the purposes and plans that He has for our lives.

We are each uniquely gifted and we are called to serve God and others with our gifts. First Peter 4:10 says, "Each one should use whatever gift he has received to serve others, faithfully administering God's grace in its various forms." Did you catch that last part? "Various."

In an article in *Today's Christian Woman* magazine, Bible teacher Dee Brestin says:

There can be so much rivalry between women. . . . But if you believe God has a unique purpose and plan for *your* life, then you can rejoice when great things happen to others around you.[3]

When I got pregnant I became aware of the many fears I had should I become the mother of a little girl. (We waited until the kids were born to find out the sex.) I became aware of the areas I lacked and the things I didn't know how to do. Things like French-braiding hair or talking to a teenager. (I didn't know what to do with myself in my teen years, and nobody else seemed to know either, so how on earth was I going to know how to talk to my own teen?) Once Grace was born, the Lord eased my fears by showing me that He had surrounded me with a circle of friends—women who loved Christ, loved me, and loved my daughter, women who each possess gifts that they generously share through friendship with me and my family. I didn't need to know how to French-braid because Grace could go see "Auntie" Heather for that. If Grace didn't want to talk to me about certain things as a teen, I could direct her to "Auntie" Andrea or "Auntie" Sue. Christ also reminded me that if I were the perfect mother, what would my daughter need a Savior for?

In *Captivating,* author Stasi Eldredge invites women to ponder the following question: "God wanted to reveal something about himself, so he gave us Eve. When you are with a woman, ask yourself, *what is she telling me about God?* It will open up wonders for you."[4]

Embracing your circle of friends, or as I put it in this chapter, "wearing your crown," has everything to do with acknowledging that you are "fearfully and wonderfully made" (Psalm 139:14), that your friends are too, and that *together* you make the world around you even more bright and more beautiful; together you crown the world with a more complete vision of who God is and what His love looks like.

Wearing the crown is saying that you don't need to be perfect and good at everything. It is saying that you need people in your life. It is allowing yourself to be inspired by the women that surround you. It is acknowledging that you are gifted in this way, and that this other gift is not yours but your sister's. This is not complacency (as some would think) but permission to be freed from your own expectations.

Read what author Valerie Monroe writes in "Life Isn't a Beauty Contest":.

> **Women can be lovely in many ways—as many ways, it seems, as there are women. It's easy to be very happy, noticing things to admire rather than looking only for ways to be admired. You know that feeling you get when you see a lush summer garden, abundantly green and fragrant and riotous with blossoms? Does it bother you that you're not as beautiful as it is? No, of course not; it's a garden. Its beauty has nothing to do with you, takes nothing away from yours. In fact, standing in the middle of a flourishing garden, filling your eyes with the deep and impossibly delicate colors, inhaling the odors, sweet and complex, you might feel more beautiful, more precious yourself, marveling at your own ability to perceive it at all. . . . A thing of beauty needs no comparison, only an eye to behold it.[5]**

Affirm the Women in Your Life . . . Tell Them How They Inspire You

> **Dare to be the singular expression of truth and beauty that God created you to be.[6]**
>
> —Brennan Manning

I, along with many others, continuously tell Liz Caddow what an inspiration she is. Liz started a school. Yes, I said a school. Liz was one of the original Monday night girls (mentioned in chapter 1), and at that time she was a junior high history teacher. She loved her job but was dissatisfied with the direction public education was taking. After she became pregnant with her first child, this sense of unease increased and she began to pray about it. Over the course of a year, it became clear to Liz that God was calling her to start a school (a classical Christian school). Our Monday night girls watched this seed of a dream begin to bloom. We *told her* that we marveled at her passion, wisdom, and obedience to the vision that God placed on her heart. With much tenacity and enthusiasm on Liz's part, what started out as an idea became a reality and, a few short years later, Trinity Classical Academy is raising up over two hundred young people (K–8 with plans to expand to 12) of virtue, purpose, wisdom, and courage.

They Might Not Know . . .

Sometimes God will use you to help friends see the gifts and vision He has placed in them. By affirming the gifts that you see in them, you have the opportunity to partner with the Holy Spirit to empower them to risk being who God intends them to be.

For years my friend Jennifer worked as an AWANA volunteer. She believed in this ministry and really wanted to be a part of it by educating her children about God and His Word. AWANA met on Wednesday evenings, and Jennifer and I (along with our friends Kathy and Gabbi) always walked Wednesday and Sunday mornings. For many months we listened to Jennifer talk about how her heart wasn't in leading AWANA anymore and how she just felt weary thinking about going to set up, but that she was torn because she really did think it was a great program that needed volunteers to function. In the meantime, the other thing Jennifer was always doing, the thing that was a natural part of her, was singing. If she was driving she was singing, and if she was walking she was singing. She was always singing. Sometimes it was some old disco song from a one-hit wonder from the '70s; sometimes it was the latest jingle for a fast-food chain—it didn't seem to matter! Most of the time Jennifer was humming or singing hymns and worship music.

Kathy, Gabbi, and I started encouraging Jennifer about her obvious gift and love of singing. We'd get on her: "When are you going to start teaching me how to play the piano?" "Why aren't you onstage with the worship team?" She'd kind of shrug her shoulders and keep walking. That didn't stop us. "Jennifer, you were meant to sing. . . . This is when you feel God's pleasure. . . . Your voice glorifies God." One day as we walked and talked about her struggle to make a decision about whether or not she should continue to volunteer with AWANA, she said, "I just want my children to be able to see me serve God." All three friends chimed in, "If you are singing with the worship team, they will not only be able to see you serve God, they will be able to see you serve Him with *gladness*."

Jennifer doesn't show up for our Sunday morning walks as much these days (we miss seeing her). Now we have to wait a few more hours to see her—until we show up at church and stand to worship the Lord. That's when we see her radiant face as she leads us all in a time of praise.

I recently had the great privilege of hearing one of my all-time favorite authors, Brennan Manning, speak about the power of affirmation and how we each possess the power to change lives by speaking words of affirmation to one another. He explained that through the power of the Holy Spirit, when we affirm people we give them "the courage to be."

Tell your friends the ways they inspire you. Affirm their God-given gifts. Let them know the ways you see God using them and rejoice in the knowledge that in so doing you are giving them "the courage to be."

Lessons From "The Greats"

We weren't jealous of one another because we knew that we all brought something different to the table.

 **Ponder**

What gifts and/or traits do you admire in your friends?

Is it difficult for you to celebrate their gifts? Why or why not?

What gifts and/or traits have your friends said they admire in you?

Was it hard to answer that question?

Did you find yourself stuck anywhere in this chapter? Did you find a place that needs the healing touch of God or the strength and courage to move forward?

 ## Pray

For you created my inmost being; you knit me together in my mother's womb. I praise you because I am fearfully and wonderfully made; your works are wonderful, I know that full well.

(Psalm 139:13–14)

Lord, you say in your Word that "I am fearfully and wonderfully made," yet I have a difficult time believing that because _____
(tell God your reasons). *Forgive me for thinking that I don't measure up. I want to believe that you love me just the way I am. Forgive me for any unbelief I have in this area; I surrender it to you and ask you to transform it. I want to celebrate the fearful and wonderful ways that you have made me. Please show me in the days and weeks to come some specific ways that you have done so. Help me to be generous with my gifts and talents. Forgive me, Lord, for comparing myself to my friends instead of celebrating my friends. Give me the eyes to see the fearful and wonderful ways that you have created them. I specifically want to thank you for* _____ (write down a friend's name and the qualities that you appreciate in her). *Help me to seize opportunities to celebrate and affirm my friend(s) with my words and with my actions. I thank you that I have the opportunity to be myself and let my friends be themselves, and that this shows the world a more complete view of who you are. In Jesus' name, amen.*

 ## Apply

The next time you see a friend, tell her one of the things you admire about her. (For example, "I love the way you delight in your children. It reminds me to laugh with my own kids.")

When a friend offers to help you, say yes. (For example, "I can show you how to do that faux finish on your wall," or "I can help you organize your closet.") Even better, ask her if she would help you with one of her talents. After sixteen years of teaching aerobics, I got two stress fractures in my foot and spent a year in and out of different kinds of casts. When I got my second plaster cast I asked my friend Michele if she would beautify my cast by using her gift of artistry on my leg. She agreed, and soon after I was walking around with a purple leg that read in lovely yellow script, "*Cast* your cares on the Lord" (Psalm 55:22).

Offer to help your friends with one of your gifts.

The next time you are asked to do a task that you are not good at or that you do not enjoy, own your limitations. ("What a compliment to be asked to be on the decorations committee for the gala! To be honest, decorating isn't my specialty; however, I would be glad to help out as a greeter that night!")

Risk being yourself and letting your light shine.

Letters From a Friend

Hello My Friend,

It was good to hear your voice. Thank you for acknowledging my accomplishment of earning my BA degree—CAN YOU BELIEVE IT?! After all these years I am finally realizing my dream. God is good.

I remember several years ago you encouraged me to read a book that taught how God wanted everyone to have the desire of their heart—it challenged the reader to pinpoint that desire and strive to make it happen. I think the name of the book was THE PATH, although I am not certain. Anyway, I never read the book. I started it—but after a chapter or two I stopped reading it. I didn't think it was a good idea for me to get excited about something (getting a degree) just to be disappointed—I was raising three sons.

My life never allowed me such a generous offer as to strive for something just for me. Don't get me wrong—I have a wonderful life. However, the path of my life was laid out for me at sixteen years old when I had David. I chose to put my children before me, and someday I would have time to do something for me. It's time—after twenty years of raising a family, I did it; God allowed me to do it, and the funny thing is, if you had asked me five or six years ago, I couldn't see the light at the end of the tunnel—I put the book down. Oh ye of little faith. . . .

I thought you would appreciate my story because—in part—you are a piece of it. Thank you.

Peace and honor to your home,

Love,
Gina

Chapter 8

Worshiping the Giver of the Crown

Remember that the crown is a gift to be received and appreciated, not worshiped.

> Things have become necessary to us, a development
> never originally intended. God's gifts now take the place
> of God, and the whole course of nature is upset by the
> monstrous substitution.[1]

—A. W. Tozer

> You were created to worship.
> Make certain you are wearing your crown but
> worshiping the Giver.

> The Lord would speak to Moses face to face, as a man
> speaks with his friend.

(Exodus 33:11)

God is up to something. He is doing something new, and I am watching in wonder as it unfolds.

After dinner two nights ago we had our traditional mini prayer session around the kitchen table. My daughter randomly selected our former neighbors' (the Bracketts) card out of the Christmas prayer basket (the place we store all the cards we get during the Christmas season so that we can pray for our friends and family throughout the year). Knowing that they were in the process of looking to buy a house, we prayed specifically for their upcoming move. We prayed that the Lord would clearly show them the home He had prepared in advance for them to live in, and that throughout this process the whole family would experience God's peace.

The next day Grace got in the car and announced, "God answered our prayers, Mom!" She went on to tell me that the Bracketts' daughter Lindsay had informed her they had put an offer on a house on Shadylane, five houses down from us!

Three years earlier the Bracketts sold their house on Shadylane—the house right next door to us. I've mentioned in previous chapters the positive impact that this particular friendship has had on our lives and how much our families were blessed by one another, which is why, after almost a decade together, we were devastated to find out they would be leaving (to build a bigger house that could accommodate Michele's parents, who would eventually live with them).

A few months following the Bracketts' move away from Shadylane, I had a spiritual epiphany of sorts. I was on a morning walk around the neighborhood when this thought rose up within me:

I would not have moved.

As I continued to let this thought roll around in my brain, I became aware that if God had *clearly* called our family to move somewhere, whether it was a job transfer for Russ, an opportunity to do mission work for a season in a foreign country, or even a country estate that was gifted to us, I would have said no, and it would have been because I was unwilling to let go of living next door to the Bracketts and the friendship that we had as a result. In that moment, on that walk, I realized that my hands were holding on too tightly to this friendship, too tightly to this crown. A gift that God had given me had begun to take precedence over His place in my life. I was worshiping the crown and not the Giver of the crown. I believe that one of the reasons the Lord took this friendship away for a season was so that He could take back His rightful place in my life. He slipped that treasured friendship from my grasp until He could become my treasure once more.

We were created to worship. Rick Warren says in his bestseller *The Purpose-Driven Life*: "Worship is a universal urge, hard-wired by God into the very fiber of our being—an inbuilt need to connect with God. Worship is as natural as eating or breathing. If we fail to worship God, we always find a substitute, even if it ends up being ourselves."[2]

We were created with a bent toward worship, and we must continually guard and check our hearts to make sure that the One we are worshiping is God. God is the One who gives us our crown of friends. *Our friends are not God* and *they are not to be worshiped*. God will never share His glory with another, and we must ask God to help us never lose sight of the fact that "every good and perfect gift is from above, coming down from the Father of the heavenly lights" (James 1:17), and praise and worship Him accordingly.

How Do You know If You're Worshiping the Crown and Not the Giver?

Are You Demanding That Your Friends Meet Your Every Need?

Men are prone to make idols out of their careers and accomplishments. Women, as the relational sex, are particularly vulnerable to making people their idols. Women can easily make their husbands, children, or friends their idols, expecting them to fill their deepest needs and to never let them down.[3]

—Dee Brestin

I clearly remember the first women's retreat I went on. It was a Friday to Saturday event held at a quaint little retreat center in the woods. There were probably fifty women there, and I was about seven months pregnant (and wearing some scary yellow leggings and a purple maternity top . . . eek!). Being pregnant was not the main reason I remember this particular retreat. What stands out in my memory is walking around feeling dissatisfied.

I remember seeing my friends looking all happy and peaceful and laughing, and I felt like they weren't paying enough attention to me. (Hang with me, because this sounds a little childish and is embarrassing to confess. Why did I agree to write this book again?) My friends weren't coming up to me and talking to me, and they weren't making sure to save me a seat at the sessions or at dinner. I felt lonely, I felt frustrated, and I didn't even know how to put all that into words at the time. I felt a longing, and I would have sworn that what I was longing for was the companionship of my friends. Looking back now I see that what I was really longing for was Christ. He was the only One who could truly satisfy my soul, and He was standing at the door and knocking LOUDLY that weekend. (See Revelation 3:20.) But I felt that if my friends would just be a little more attentive and loving toward me, I would be happy.

It was a week or two after this retreat that I asked Jesus to be my Lord and Savior. A group of women who attended the retreat gathered for coffee to follow up on our time together. My friend Sue asked the group if we all knew beyond a shadow of a doubt where we would spend eternity if we were to die today. I thought to myself, *I'm pretty sure I'm going to heaven. After all, I'm a good person, I'm a hard worker, I try to do the right thing.* My friend then asked if there was a day that we could look back on and say, "That day I know I prayed to receive Jesus Christ into my heart and asked Him to be Lord of my life." To that question, I knew the answer was no. There was not a specific day. My friend then read these words from the Bible: "If you confess with your mouth, 'Jesus is Lord,' and believe in your heart that God raised him from the dead, you will be saved" (Romans 10:9). Sue explained that it is not enough just to believe, you need to *do* something about it. You need to *receive* Jesus personally into your heart. You need to *invite Him in through prayer*. She led a prayer that day, and I prayed silently in my heart along with her. That day marked the beginning of a remarkable transformation.

Once I realized that I didn't need to work harder but that I was loved and forgiven because what Jesus had done on the cross was enough, I experienced *freedom and peace* like never before. Grace took on a whole new meaning—the beauty of the free gift that Jesus extended to me (and all those who choose to receive Him) truly became a treasure to me.

While I would like to say I was immediately carried to a place where I never placed unreasonable demands on my friends to meet all my needs, I can't. It was (and is) a learning process, a sometimes painful learning process. But one thing I know now is that when I'm feeling dissatisfied or frustrated by people, I need to ask the Lord what it is I am truly longing for; most of the time it is Him. "What a man desires is unfailing love" (Proverbs 19:22).

How about you? Do you have that assurance? Do you have that experience of freedom, peace, and unfailing love?

"He loves me, He loves me not . . . ." This is usually one of the first images that comes to mind when you think of a daisy . . . sitting in a field somewhere thinking of a boy you have a crush on and plucking petals off one by one to find out if fate will have you together or not. Have you ever figuratively sat plucking petals and wondering, *Does God love me?* Wondering if the God of the universe could possibly love someone like you, someone who has made mistakes, gotten mad, screwed up big time, let people down. . . . Have you wondered if God could love you even if you stopped working so hard? The truth is that He can and He does. God's Word says, "But God demonstrates his own love for us in this: While we were still sinners, Christ died for us" (Romans 5:8). When it comes to the Lord Jesus Christ, you need not wonder, you need not play childish games or work hard to prove that you are lovable. No matter how many petals you pluck off, when it comes to Jesus and your heavenly Father, you will always end up with the truth:

He loves me.

I have learned that Jesus is my best friend and He will meet my needs. I need to rely on Him first, and then the pressure to have a friend to meet my needs becomes secondary, which frees me up to enjoy friendship even more.

—Patti

Do You Feel the Pressure to Meet All of Your Friends' Needs?

> Each of us must learn to deal with our loneliness in order to be a close friend to another. Otherwise we will choke the life out of our closest friendships by clinging and demanding too much and then be angry when our friends refuse to meet our expectations. Those who failed to receive adequate parental love and nurture in childhood need to recognize that they will be prone to greater loneliness as adults than people whose needs were adequately met.[4]
>
> —Brenda Hunter, PhD

Do you have a scene that flashes in your memory and you just know it impacted you on many levels even though you were not aware of all of them at the time? Mine is the scene of my first dance recital. I was eight years old and had been taking a jazz class once a week for a year and was now going to be in my first onstage performance. I don't remember the song I danced to, but I sure do remember the outfit. It was a real winner . . . a dark green tank leotard with gold sequins, tan tights, and Keds from Kmart that my mom spray-painted gold. Nice. I don't remember much about my time on the stage. What I do remember is running out to the audience after the performance to see my parents and discovering that the chair next to my mother was empty. "Dad had to work late," Mom explained.

I think that moment marked the first (but not the last) time I ever truly felt let down. It was a cut that went so deep it caused me to make an unspoken promise to myself: "I will NEVER let anybody down." An unreasonable demand for a little girl—an unreasonable demand for a big girl—but a demand I placed on myself nonetheless. Love became synonymous with "I will be there for them." "Them" being my girlfriends, my husband, my children, and whoever else I sensed needed me.

I lived with a lot of pressure in the friend department because of this promise (and my illusion of power). So much so that I journaled and prayed about it regularly:

I'm afraid I'll fail at being what she needs.

Will I do enough? Say enough?
Be quiet at the right time? Speak the truth at the right time?
Will I be enough?

I can't be everything she needs.

I'm afraid of the day I fail her. Will she hate me? Leave me? Accuse me?

Will I stand accused?
I will if I buy in to the fact that I need to be more than I am.

I am enough.
I love well.
The love I give is enough.
The love I give is good, beautiful, and my best.

I am Abba's child.
I belong to my dad.
He loves through me.
His love is good, great . . . delicious.
His love meets deep needs.

I give you this pressure I feel, Jesus. I surrender it to you.
I admit, confess, own that I am not you nor do I want to be you.
I am a girl that loves you and that wants to honor you in her relationships.
I can't be honoring to you by carrying this burden, so I cast this burden on you, Lord.
I ask that you replace this pressure with peace.

I stand before you . . . "enough."

Love,
Your Girl, Tracy

Psalm 121:1-2 says, "Where does my help come from? My help comes from the Lord, the Maker of heaven and earth." God *could* choose to meet needs through people (the topic of this book). However, He *could* also choose *not* to use people. Am I willing to entrust not only my needs to my heavenly Father but my friends' needs as well? Am I willing to trust that He will meet their needs even if *I'm* not the one He uses to meet them?

Are Your Friends Getting Your Best?

Are you placing more of a priority on seeing your friends or meeting your friends' needs than you are on your time with God, your husband, your children, your work . . . ? Who is getting your best?

Years ago I went through a terrific time of training called "CLASS" (Christian Leaders Authors and Speakers Services). At the end of the training, my small-group leader sat me down privately and said these words to me: "Tracy, you have a natural gift for speaking, and I can see you having success in this field in the future. *However,* you need to know that with children as young as yours, your *primary ministry* right now is at home with your family."

These words had a tremendous impact on me. Although they were given to me in more of a career guidance setting, they have caused me to repeatedly ask myself the question, "Who is getting my best?"

If you are giving your best to your friends and the leftovers to God, your husband, children, job/ministry, you could be worshiping the crown and not the Giver.

But seek first his kingdom and his righteousness, and all these things will be given to you as well.

(Matthew 6:33)

Are You More Concerned With What Your Friends Think Than What God Thinks?

Who are you living to please?

Is it more important for you to keep your friends thinking well of you than to do what you know you are being called to do?

As I've mentioned several times throughout this book, I grew up with a deep need to be liked by everyone. So you can probably imagine that the thought of having a person out there clearly not liking me could be catastrophic.

A few years into having close, growing, Christ-centered relationships, a situation such as this arose. I began to have a growing sense that one of my friends clearly had issues with me and didn't really like being around me. While we did attempt to work through these issues on several occasions, it became clear that this dynamic was not going to change overnight. I believe that we both trusted the Lord would work out our situation in time. However, in the immediacy, I was left with the deep sense that there was someone in my life who didn't like me, and it shook me to the core.

It also made me aware that I was more outwardly focused than was healthy. I had a radar sense for how other people felt, and I would respond accordingly. This radar helped me extend empathy and compassion toward people who needed it. But it also caused me to more often than not disregard my personal feelings and value the thoughts and feelings of others more than my own. Even worse, this radar caused me to be more tuned in to people than to the Holy Spirit. The Lord used the dynamic in this particular friendship to begin a refining work in me. During the weeks and months that followed, it was as though God kept asking me, "Is it enough that I (your heavenly Father) love you (1 John 4:10), approve you (Jeremiah 1:5), and promise never to leave you (Hebrews 13:5)? Is that enough? Am I enough for you, Tracy?"

When you get to the place where you can give a wholehearted yes to those godly questions, then you will begin to live for an "audience of One."

If you are aware that people-pleasing is an area that you struggle with, know that while it is possible for God to do a miraculous work in you and remove this desire for man's approval from you, it is more likely to be something that you will have to pray about regularly and talk through consistently. It may be the thing that keeps you at the foot of the cross, and really, isn't that the point?

A few years ago Brennan Manning said one sentence that was so radical to me it has never left me (and I hope it never leaves you): "You are always being gazed at with infinite tenderness." God loves you, likes you, and is with you always. Worship Him accordingly.

> **"Never will I leave you; never will I forsake you."** So we say with confidence, **"The Lord is my helper; I will not be afraid. What can man do to me?"**
>
> (Hebrews 13:5-6)

The Radical Truth

Are you ready for some radical truth? The following verse never ceases to amaze me. It literally makes me shake my head in wonder. In John 15:9, Jesus tells us, "As the Father has loved me, so have I loved you."

How are you doing? Are you shaking your head yet? Isn't that radical? If you're not amazed, you might need to hear it again: The way that God (Almighty, Awesome, All-Holy, All-Powerful God) loves His Son Jesus Christ is the same way that Christ loves you!

Please take note that it does *not* say, "That's how I will love you when you get your act together," or "That's how I would have loved you if you hadn't made so many stupid decisions." NO. It says, "As the Father has loved me, so have I loved you."

Jesus loves you, and He goes on in this verse to tell you the path to true joy—everlasting, never-ending joy. In light of the way that Jesus loves us, He says, "Now remain in my love. If you obey my commands, you will remain in my love, just as I have obeyed my Father's commands and remain in his love. I have told you this so that my joy may be in you and that your joy may be complete. My command is this: Love each other as I have loved you. . . . You are my friends if you do what I command. I no longer call you servants, because a servant does not know his master's business. Instead, I have called you friends, for everything that I learned from my Father I have made known to you" (John 15:9-15).

Jesus not only loves you, He calls you "friend." Remain in a state of awe of the radical truth that Jesus loves you, that you are His, that you will spend eternity with Him, and that nothing can ever separate you from His love. Pray for a sense of wonder, pray for a sense of awe, pray for the ability to consistently worship the true Savior, the only One who can truly satisfy, and pray that Christ would help you to follow His command to "love each other" and guard your heart from worshiping others.

An Illustration of Worshiping the Giver and Not the Crown

Delight yourself in the Lord and he will give you the desires of your heart.

(Psalm 37:4)

On one occasion a few years ago my friend Andrea and I went on an overnighter to Palm Springs. It was an all-expense-paid recognition trip for her and her husband (a commercial real estate agent who is also a Pac-Ten basketball referee). The trip happened to land in the middle of basketball season so Andrea's husband couldn't go, and he suggested she take the trip with a girlfriend (that would be me—yay!).

Andrea and I left for Palm Springs on Friday night from Los Angeles, which meant two words: *major traffic*. Then it began to rain so the two-hour car ride took four, and by the time we got to the hotel it was late. Upon checking in at the front desk we discovered two facts: This was the hotel where the recently televised *Bachelorette* wedding extravaganza had taken place, and because we were checking in so late there weren't very many rooms left to choose from.

It seemed as though we were back to doing the Avon 3-Day on the way to our room. We walked down at least five different *long* hallways before the bellhop finally stopped the cart in front of our door. We stepped into a chandeliered entryway. Yes, I said entryway! Off the entryway was a beautiful marble "guest" bathroom. As we continued walking, we found ourselves in a living room complete with sofa, chairs, coffee tables, television, and a *grand piano*. To the right of the living room was a dining room complete with china cabinets, a large oval table, and chairs for an intimate dinner for eight. To the left of the living room was the master bedroom with the biggest, fluffiest bed you've ever laid eyes on. Off of the bedroom was another giant marble bathroom that had four separate rooms attached to it: a room for the enormous Jacuzzi tub, a room with two sit-down vanities, a room for the toilet area, and a walk-in closet. When the bellhop said "This was the only room we had left; will it do?" we responded immediately by doing cartwheels down the length of the living room (I am serious). I think we scared the bellhop because he made a quick exit, stage left.

This is an example of how you can know if you are worshiping the Giver versus worshiping the crown. If my friendship with Andrea was what I was worshiping, at that moment I would have felt the pressure to make her know that she is the most amazing friend in the entire world to have even invited me to stay with her. I might have also felt the pressure to make it up to her and think of some extravagant way that I could express my appreciation for her. Instead, once the bellhop left, Andrea and I looked at each other in amazement and said, "How much does God love us?" We realized simultaneously that it was God who wanted to treat us so extravagantly. It made us giggle (and take out our cameras) to think that our God delighted in us that much.

God loves us all, and in His generous love and care for us He provides beautiful gifts that sometimes come packaged in the form of a close friendship. Let us make sure that we continue to worship the true treasure and not the gifts from His hands.

I knew Christ personally when our friendship with the Bracketts came into the life of our family. I even prayed prayers of thanksgiving countless times regarding the special bond between us. However, over a period of time, in subtle ways, this relationship began to take a place in my heart that only God wanted to occupy. And so, I believe, He took it away for a time. I now thank God, the Giver of all good gifts, for the gift of friendship that He is bringing back not only into my life, but into the life of my family.

Let us all pray that God would help us live lives that worship Him and that recognize Him as our true treasure.

 Ponder

Who do you call first in times of crisis? In times of celebration? In times of sorrow?

Of the four sections in this chapter (Are you demanding that your friends meet your every need? Do you feel the pressure to meet all your friends' needs? Are your friends getting your best? Are you more concerned with what your friends think than what God thinks?), which resonated with you the most? Do you think it is an area of vulnerability for you? Why?

Have you ever felt God was calling you to do or say something that one of your friends might disapprove of? What did you do? How did you handle that situation?

Who gets your best? Who do you spend the most time and energy with?

If you were to die today, do you know where you would spend eternity?

Is there a day that you can look back on and know that you received Christ as your personal Savior?

What is keeping you from receiving God's gift of grace?

Did you find yourself stuck anywhere in this chapter? Did you find a place that needs the healing touch of God or the strength and courage to move forward?

Pray

Father God, I ask that you would guard my heart against worshiping anybody or anything other than you. You alone are worthy of my worship. In your Word you tell me, "Those who cling to worthless idols forfeit the grace that could be theirs" (Jonah 2:8). Show me if I am clinging to anything other than you. Loosen my grip so that I have open hands to receive the grace that comes from you alone. Hold my chin gently in your hand that my eyes might look deeply and constantly into yours. For I know that when I gaze into your eyes I will truly know that you, Christ, are not only the Giver of all gifts, but that you are more than enough for me. In Jesus' name, amen.

Apply

Before you get out of bed tomorrow, lie there quietly and thank God for loving you. In those quiet moments before the day starts, worship Him for who He is.

The next time a friend does something nice for you or says something nice to you, quietly thank God for working through this individual to show you His love.

If today is the day that you would like to receive Jesus Christ as your Savior, and in doing so worship the true Giver and not simply the crown, then pray with me:

Father God, thank you for the treasure, Jesus Christ, who died for my sins so that I could be forgiven, and rose from the dead so that I could have eternal life. I open the door of my heart this very minute and invite Jesus to come in. I receive His gift of forgiveness and eternal life gratefully. Thank you for your Holy Spirit, who has now come to live in me. Transform me, Jesus; I am yours. In Jesus' name, amen.

Letters From a Friend

My Friend,

I sensed something was troubling you at the park yesterday. I'm sorry we were not in a good place to really talk. I pray that God's peace comforts you this week and that the truth of His Word encourages you.

Bless you!
Liz

Chapter 9

Uprooted and Transplanted

When a friendship transitions because of relocation . . .

Some flowers are right in front of us so we see them constantly, while other flowers are behind us. We may not see them as often, but they are an integral part of our crown—beautiful, binding, and backing us all the way.

A friend is always a friend, but we do need to make new friends because we need friends *close by* in our lives.

—Jean

I met her within hours of her move onto our street. She suddenly appeared in my neighbors' yard to play; her name as new to me as the girl herself. Corry had shoulder-length blond hair and huge brown eyes. She was the most beautiful girl I had ever seen. I soon came to admire her sense of style—denim bell-bottoms and coordinating tops—and her sense of adventure. Together we would leap off the swing set like the Bionic Woman (Lindsay Wagner), run down the block like two of Charlie's Angels, and ward off flying bullets with our silver bracelets like Wonder Woman (these bracelets were created by wrapping flexible aluminum rulers around our wrists). We shared a love for music—marching up and down the sidewalk singing songs from *The Brady Bunch*—and we spent hours in the summer watching dandelion stems curl into delicate shapes when dropped into puddles. We were six years old, living on Arden Street in Sault Ste. Marie, Ontario.

Corry became my very first best friend, and I was certain that we'd remain that close forever. Life, however, had different plans, and on a cold, gray day a new word entered my vocabulary: *divorce*. Corry's life would be permanently altered, and mine would be forever changed as my best friend moved away. The move was not radical in terms of distance (a fifteen-minute drive across town), but when you're used to opening a screen door and running into the arms of your girlfriend, it was horribly absolute.

A flower had fallen out of my daisy chain, but it felt more like it had been ripped away, and I, well, I felt as though I was dangling, unsure of what to hold on to anymore. I was not the one who had moved away, I was the one who was left. I don't recall using the term *best friend* again, at least not until recently, and I don't recall being left like that again either, at least not until recently.

In the years that followed Corry's move, I was the friend who moved away. It was I who started at new schools and learned the names of the new faces that lined the street. I did the leaving. I made the most of these moves, calling them "adventures" and "fresh starts." Perhaps this gave me a sense of control, or perhaps because of losing my friend Corry, I preferred to keep friends at a comfortable distance so that in case of sudden change I need not spend much time dangling from a broken chain.

I have come to realize in recent years that whether we are the friend who moves to a new town (we've been transplanted) or we are the friend who remains (with a life that has been uprooted), there is grief, there is transition, and there are choices to be made.

In working on this chapter, I consulted several women who have experienced being transplanted (moving away) or having their lives uprooted (remaining while their friends moved away) as adults. For this reason, in this chapter you will find many more collections of thoughts and quotes. I hope they are helpful to you.

> **Friendships transition and enter new phases even when all we do is move to a different part of town, and that is because the "intersections of your life" have changed. I recently moved to a more rural side of town and have discovered that I need to be very intentional about making new friends that live close by. Even though it's just thirty miles away, I don't see my long-time friends quite as often as I used to.**
>
> —Marita Littauer, coauthor of *Wired That Way*

Breaking the News

If you are the friend who is moving away, ask the Lord to help you in every aspect of communicating this news to your friends, including how much information you should initially share.

Since this news may be a surprise to your friend, try not to be shocked if she has a difficult time at first listening to your reasons for leaving and/or your feelings. She is processing new information, which you've had a little more time to digest. As the days go by, try to schedule time together to talk through feelings and to ask from her/them what you might need (support, encouragement, prayers) in the weeks to come.

> **I knew the move was the best decision for our family, but I was so very sad to leave the friends that had become my best girlfriends.**
>
> —Lindsey

> **After initially shrieking "NO!" my friends asked me questions to make sure they understood what my motivation was for moving. I had many conversations with many friends. Sometimes I felt like I had to prove or convince why it was important and the right decision for me to move.**
>
> —Patti

Sharing Your Heart

If you just found out your friend is leaving, you now have a decision to make. Will you tell your girlfriend how you are feeling? I believe that honesty and authenticity are key in any healthy relationship; however, I also believe it is important to bathe these conversations in prayer. Ask the Lord to examine your heart, and watch over the timing of these conversations. I encourage you to ask yourself, "What is my motivation in sharing my feelings with her?"

Is it . . .

- to let her know how much she means to me and that I will miss her?
- to make her feel guilty and let her know she is ruining my life?
- to change her mind and make her want to stay?
- to sabotage our relationship so that I don't have to feel the pain?
- to be honest so that if she senses I am acting or behaving differently she knows that I am doing the best I can—in pain, but committed to the friendship?

When a friend tells you she's moving away, your heart may sink and you may feel devastated. Talk it out with her.

—Patti

I still think that it is easier to say things than to un-say things. Much of what I felt, and still feel, is clearly between me and God to work through. I don't think it would have been helpful for me to express to her everything I was thinking and feeling. We just tried to be as positive and supportive as we could be without being phony. I knew she would bloom where she was planted; that's the kind of person she is. I prayed for them, prayed for me, and held tight to God's promises that He would work everything out. Without the knowledge that I did not need to be in control of everything (because God is), I think I could have really damaged the friendship we had.

—Elizabeth

My best friend was disappointed and sad but understood that I had to go.

—Tammy

Coping With Feelings of Loss

Feeling the Feelings

As I was making dinner the phone rang. When I picked it up I heard the familiar sound of Rob's voice say, "Yo, Tracy!" (his traditional greeting). I promptly burst into tears and am fairly certain that I royally freaked the man out, because I have never quite heard that degree of panic enter my former next-door neighbor's voice. He went into this nervous tailspin. "It's okay, Tracy, we'll still see each other, I mean, like, I'm coming over with Michele and the kids tomorrow to get something. . . ." Through my tears I replied, "It's okay, Rob. I'm sorry, it's just that I miss you guys already and it's only been a few days since you've moved."

Anytime you experience significant loss, it is important to give yourself permission to grieve. Journal your feelings; be honest and vulnerable in prayer. Allow yourself to have a process and to take the time to walk through the process. It will probably take a little time. Yes, the Lord is doing something new, and yes, we are to have faith and remain flexible, but it is okay to cry some tears and even admit that you are angry. Your feelings will not cause God to fall off His throne!

> **I didn't want to move at all! I don't like change and felt very nervous, anxious, and fearful. I was a little resentful, also, toward my husband. The move was for his work.**
>
> —Tammy

> **I went through a lot of emotions—disappointment (that God could give me the best friend ever only to yank her away); anger (toward her and her husband for moving); self-pity; wanting to change their minds; disliking myself for the bitterness I felt. After I got through being mad, I was really depressed. I felt so lonely and fearful. I geared up for a long season of being by myself, doing things alone, not having anyone to really open up to. I remember most days just feeling that tightness in my throat—the one that comes when you're trying to hold back tears. That was there every day. But even through**

that I just kept praying that God would change my heart. Through the tears and anger and lonely times I kept coming back to God, trusting Him with the emotions I could barely acknowledge to myself, let alone share with another person.

—Elizabeth

Clinging to God

Change has never been easy for me. With a father who suffered from depression, I was somewhat traumatized by abrupt change growing up. As an adult, this trauma translated itself into an ominous feeling that when life seemed to be going well, the other shoe could drop at any moment. Because of this childhood wound, one of God's character traits that I have found to be incredibly healing is that He is "immutable," which is defined in Webster's as "not capable of or susceptible to change."[1] A Scripture verse that clearly communicates this concept is found in Hebrews 13:8: "Jesus Christ is the same yesterday and today and forever."

When a change comes your way, whether it is in a friendship or in any other area of your life, cling to the One who never changes. Stand on the solid ground of His promises. Here is a list of promises compiled by women who have been uprooted and transplanted. These verses helped these women stand firm and are sure to be an encouragement to you as you make your way through this time of transition.

"For I know the plans I have for you," declares the Lord, "plans to prosper you and not to harm you, plans to give you hope and a future."

(Jeremiah 29:11)

And we know that in all things God works for the good of those who love him, who have been called according to his purpose.

(Romans 8:28)

I will never leave you nor forsake you.

(Joshua 1:5)

Therefore, since we are receiving a kingdom that cannot be shaken, let us be thankful, and so worship God acceptably with reverence and awe.

(Hebrews 12:28)

A friend loves at all times.

(Proverbs 17:17)

And my God will meet all your needs according to his glorious riches in Christ Jesus.

(Philippians 4:19)

Delight yourself in the Lord and he will give you the desires of your heart.

(Psalm 37:4)

No discipline seems pleasant at the time, but painful. Later on, however, it produces a harvest of righteousness and peace for those who have been trained by it.

(Hebrews 12:11)

Moving a lot (four places in one year) taught me to trust God a lot more than I may have before.

—Brenda

Sending a Daisy Off With Love

In God's Word we are called to make a "sacrifice of praise" (Hebrews 13:15). The word *sacrifice* communicates that in all likelihood it will be quite challenging and possibly even painful. Can you remember a time when the last thing you felt like doing was to sing praises to the Lord? We praise God because He is worthy of our praise and because we trust His holy Word even when it hurts. Sometimes we are called to act in loving ways even when it hurts. Sending a friend off with love can be just one of those occasions.

When Michele and Rob moved, I wept for weeks beforehand . . . and they knew it. I was so sad to see them go and to let go of the dreams I had of watching our kids traverse the teen years together.

I'd envisioned Michele and I holding each other up while Lauren and Spencer learned to drive. I'd imagined taking pictures of Lindsay and Grace in their prom dresses in the front yard. But the day came when the moving truck showed up and what I needed to do was to call on God to give me the strength to help them pack boxes and load up the truck. God called me to send them off with a "sacrifice of love."

How can you send your daisy off with a "sacrifice of love"? Pray and ask the Lord to show you ways that you can be a blessing during this transition time.

My friends are so amazing because they are all so committed to Christ. They prayed for me, brought me coffee when I was feeling down, helped me pack, threw me a party, and continued to support our decision even when the timing felt wrong. They are truly the most amazing friends!

—Lindsey

Staying Connected With the Daisies Who Are Far Away

Just because you no longer share the day-in, day-out activities of life does not mean that you will be unable to maintain a meaningful friendship. What it does mean is that you will need to get creative, flexible, and intentional about staying connected.

If your friendship is in God's will, nothing can destroy it. Things may be hard, but with prayer and perseverance on both parts, it can be better than you ever imagined.

—Patti

Here are a couple of creative ways to stay connected following a move:

My friend Tina and I had an instant connection the first time we met and are still soul mates. However, God moved her family to Colorado a few years ago so we've

lived far apart for several years. Still, we always know
when the other one needs a call or a note . . . praise the
Lord for the Holy Spirit's prompting us to call each other
or write at just the right time!

—Dena Dyer, author of *Groovy Chicks' Road Trip to Peace*

Dream together and hold each other accountable for
making those dreams a reality. Share books, notes, and
studies together. Keep in communication and
ask God to keep you close in spirit.

—Lindsey

Growing Pains and Gains

When I look back over my life, I can't help but notice that the
times I grew the most spiritually and emotionally were the times of
my greatest pain and discomfort. These stretches of suffering caused
me to press in closer to my God and to get to know Him in deeper
ways. I do not understand why times of suffering result in growth; I
just know that God's Word teaches us that "suffering produces perseverance; perseverance, character; and character, hope. And hope
does not disappoint us, because God has poured out his love into our
hearts by the Holy Spirit, whom he has given us" (Romans 5:3–5).
Listen to the hope that a few sisters in Christ discovered after their
daisy chains were changed as a result of a move:

I have grown so much. Contrary to what I thought would
happen, I'm less lonely now than I've ever been. I've
learned to hold my friends with "open arms," knowing that nothing is guaranteed. I've learned that my
friends will hurt my feelings, and I will hurt theirs, and
that doesn't mean we're not good friends, just that
we're people. I've learned to invest myself deeply and
in a meaningful way to many friends instead of pouring
everything into one friend. I've learned to be grateful
for the life situation the Lord has provided for my family.
And I've learned to have compassion for my friend who
moved, who is dealing with her own life situation and trying to do what's best for her family. I have also learned

to be more joyful in life. Things will change, so enjoy what's here today and be thankful for it.

—Elizabeth

After I moved, my relationship with Christ deepened to a new level. I realized I was relying on friends to meet most of my emotional needs, and Jesus was asking me to turn to Him to meet them. It was a hard season but God was pruning me. As soon as I surrendered to this, I quickly learned that God was still growing my friendships while He was growing me. My girlfriends are still my best friends, and my relationship with Jesus has grown by leaps and bounds. God clearly takes away sometimes to produce fruit within us. It doesn't always make sense, but I've learned that I can always trust Him even when I can't understand.

—Lindsey

Lessons From "The Greats"

Life brings change even to friendships. It is important not to resist the change but to go with the flow and continue to work at your relationships.

Where to Look for New Daisies

At some point following your arrival in a new community it will be time to gather your bouquet once again. This may happen sooner than later like it did for my older sister, Nancy:

When I moved back to Reno after my grandpa's funeral, I found a new friend in my across-the-street neighbor. My mom pulled up the U-Haul, and a gal shouted from her porch, "Do you need any help?" "No," I said, and then I opened the door to the truck and my television fell facedown and smashed into bits. . . . Leslie came over and helped unload the rest of the truck, and we've been friends ever since. Clearly, I needed help!

Or it may happen a little later. After moving, Lindsey and Brenda discovered that they needed to "go outside and play" again . . . intentionally seeking out environments where flowers bloom:

> **I joined a MOPS group and have begun to make friends there. Other moms' groups and church are also a great way to get involved and seek relationships.**
>
> —Lindsey

> **GET INVOLVED! Find a church—join the choir, a Bible study, or some other group there. If you have school-age children get involved in their school and sports activities.**
>
> —Brenda

Whether friends come to you or you go looking for them, you can rest in the fact that God is your true provider. He is able and willing to meet every need that you have. Pour out your heart to Him and wait patiently and expectantly for Him to meet your relational needs. In the meantime, it might be encouraging to take a quick glance back at chapter 3.

Relational Relocation

As of late we have lived in the same town and attended the same church for many years, and while only a handful of friends have moved away geographically, many friends have moved on in other ways. I wrote this prayer one morning when I thought about the impact these friends who relocated relationally have made in my life. I hope it encourages you as you bid farewell to some of the daisies in your neighborhood.

> **Leaving**
> **As you leave, please know that I will pray for you . . .**
> **That God's love would be made real and Christ's perseverance true**
> **As you leave, please know that I will hope for you . . .**

**That daily you will rise to mercies that are new
As I stay, I choose to remember you . . .
And the way my life was blessed when you came
walking through.**

Ponder

What is the first memory you have of moving or having a friend move away?

How do you think that experience shaped the way you currently relate to friends?

How do you stay in touch with friends who no longer live close to you?

Did you find yourself stuck anywhere in this chapter? Did you find a place that needs the healing touch of God or the strength and courage to move forward?

Pray

Lord, I know that you always have my best interests at heart, but I confess that right now I feel _____ (tell God how you are feeling) *because I don't want to lose this friendship through relocation. I surrender this relationship to you, Lord, knowing that you are the One who brought us together in the first place. I entrust my friend(s) into your care and I ask you to help me in the days and weeks ahead to walk in your ways. Help me to love my friend(s) with my words and actions, help me to be honest and ask for what I need, and most of all help me keep my heart and mind open to what the future holds. For I know that your plans are to prosper me and not to harm me, plans to give me hope and a future.* (See Jeremiah 29:11.)

 ## Apply

Write a letter to your friend(s) and tell them some of your favorite shared memories (include as many details as possible) and your hopes for the future of your friendship.

E-mail a few photos of the family and ask your friend to do the same. Print those photos out and put them on the fridge. When you open the fridge say a blessing for your friend.

Get a date on the calendar to reconnect, either with a short trip or even a time you can have coffee together while you talk on the phone. Maybe this can be a regular occurrence: Wednesday nights at 8:30, for instance, you each make a cup of tea or coffee and visit for twenty minutes on the phone.

Plan a family vacation together . . . you may not get to see each other weekly, but perhaps you can start a new tradition and go to the beach together in the summer.

Check out the book *After the Boxes Are Unpacked—Moving On After Moving* by Susan Miller (Tyndale House Publishers).

If there was a verse that spoke to your heart in the "Clinging to God" section of this chapter, write it out on a file card and keep it with you. Throughout the week pull it out, meditate on it, and speak it out loud so that its promise and power can take root in your heart.

Ask the Lord to open your eyes to the people who move to your neighborhood, church, or school, so that you can be available to be used by God to help them feel welcomed. Even a warm smile and "I hope you find as much joy here as I have" will go a long way.

Letters From a Friend

She gave this name to the Lord who spoke to her: "You are the God who sees me," for she said, "I have now seen the One who sees me" (Genesis 16:13).

Dear Friend,

He sees your pain, your need, and knows you! I know you already know that, but sometimes I feel helpless when my friends are in pain, pain that I can't fully know or help them with.

I turned to this Scripture today and thought of you. I'm so grateful to know God can handle everything you need and I can just love you, pray for you, and trust His goodness toward you.

Love,
Gabbi

Chapter 10

Seasons of Friendship

Remain flexible with the changing of the seasons.

Friends are like flowers: some are annuals, brought into our lives to brighten our gardens for a season, and then they pass away, so that there is room for other flowers in our garden. Now and then God brings a perennial—who will be there season after season—but it is sometimes hard for us to know, in our limited vision, if a friend is an annual or a perennial.[1]

—Dee Brestin

Blessed is the woman that is content in the season she is in![2]

Just as daisies only grow in certain seasons and therefore can only be made into chains at certain times of the year, so do friendships have certain seasons. These seasons may be dictated by circumstance, a season of life, or even a spiritual season.

When I look back over the last dozen years, I can see that the Lord worked through people in a mighty way to bring healing to many areas of my life. God surrounded me with believers who came alongside me, opened up to me, loved me with words and actions, and lived life with me. In doing so they made Christ real to me. But there came a time when God called me to himself in a new way. There came a season when the Lord called me to come away with Him in more solitary and private ways.

In Beth Moore's *Breaking Free*[3] study, she teaches about Enoch, who is mentioned only a couple of times in the Bible. His name literally means "to be taught, discipled; narrowing," and in Genesis 5:22, it says that "Enoch walked with God 300 years." Later, in Hebrews 11, it says that Enoch "pleased God" (v. 5). Beth teaches that as believers we go through seasons of narrowing. While at other times on our spiritual journey activities, actions, and relationships were more broad and acceptable, there comes a time when our path narrows and we, like Enoch, are called to walk even more closely with God and in so doing please God. Beth teaches this concept in conjunction with Matthew 11:28-30, where we are called to be "yoked" to Jesus:

> **Come to me, all you who are weary and burdened, and I will give you rest. Take my yoke upon you and learn from me, for I am gentle and humble in heart, and you will find rest for your souls. For my yoke is easy and my burden is light.**

The first time I went through this study I was aware that I was at the beginning of a time of narrowing. The road was getting narrower and, for a season, where there had once been room for several companions, friends, and comrades to surround me, there was now beginning to be just enough room for me to walk with my Lord. In preparing to write this chapter about "Seasons of Friendship," I pulled those tapes out once again. As I listened, what struck me anew was that if the only legacy I left, if the only thing people remembered me by, if the only thing my children recalled about me was that I (like Enoch) was a woman who "walked with God," that would indeed be enough for me.

During my season of narrowing, the Lord taught me that *He* is my *best friend*. It wasn't that I was being negatively influenced by my friends; after all, God had really used these friendships as instruments of His grace, love, and healing in my life. No, God was simply calling me to a different level of intimacy with himself and with my husband.

The small group that my husband and I had been involved with on a weekly basis for eight years ended as did the Monday night women's group (aka "The Ya-Ya's"). These groups did not end badly or because of some great crisis, it just became to clear to us (as a group) that our time, for now, had run its course. We continue to remain close with the members of these groups. As a matter of fact, this is the letter that one of the Monday girls gave to each of us on the night of our last meeting:

My Monday Ya-Ya's[4]

Healing,
Provoking
Love sown
Grace given

Laughter,
Loyalty,
Confronting,
Caring,
Nurturing,
Maturing,
Silence,
Fears,
Struggle,
Tears,

Healing,
Provoking
Love spent,
Grace gained.

The sowing, the growing
And by and by, the knowing.

The beginning.
The end.
The beginning . . .

I am glad I spent my Mondays with you.
Love,
Sue

Through this narrowing time I became increasingly aware of my desire to support my husband with my words and my actions, and I also became aware at a gut level that "Where Russ goes, I go!" Whereas before I might have taken Russ more for granted or spent more time complaining about the things I wished he did differently, I now felt profoundly appreciative of the man that the Lord had hand-selected for me. I see in retrospect that God used this season of narrowing to draw us to each other and to himself in preparation for a major decision that we would be called to make a few years later—to go into full-time ministry.

During this season I also felt that God wanted me to call upon Him *first* in *every* situation and to find my satisfaction in *Him alone*. The thought of this at first felt very lonely to me, and since I am an extrovert and feel energized by people, I doubted that I would feel that sense of satisfaction. But by the end of this season I learned that the friends the Lord has given me have been a gift from His hand, and they must be appreciated as such. The gift of friendship He offers me through my husband is a gift from His hand, and it must be nurtured constantly. Most important, friendship with God himself is the true desire of my heart, and it does indeed satisfy.

On my birthday during that season of narrowing, a girlfriend gave me the gift of the classic devotional *Streams in the Desert*.[5] That evening I turned to read the selection for my birthday (August 18) and found Deuteronomy 32:12, "The Lord alone led him," followed by a beautiful poem about the blessing of walking closely with God. In blue ink in the margin of that devotional I wrote: "Lord, I thank you for everything . . . this season you've called me to walk with you alone. It is sweet and peaceful." (2004–2005)

What kind of a season are your friendships in right now?

Is it a time of great joy and love? If so, embrace, nurture, and receive that season for the blessing that it is.

Is it a time of narrowing, a time where God is calling you to spend less time with your friends and more time with Him? If so, embrace, nurture, and receive that season for the blessing that it is.

If this season feels painful, I encourage you to pour out your heart to Christ in prayer. Be honest—brutally honest. Listen to the psalmist: "You have taken my companions and loved ones from me; the darkness is my closest friend" (88:18).

It's okay to bring your anger, tears, and questions to Him. After all, that's the point. God wants your heart, and He wants to be in relationship with you. God always has your best interests at heart, for He is not only King of Kings and Lord of Lords, He calls you friend (John 15:15).

> **I remember when I first moved I felt like everything in my life had been "uprooted!" It certainly felt uncomfortable, and I admit that I questioned why God would remove all my friendships that were grounded in Him. He has taught me that He in fact did not remove them; He just changed them. I've never been one to like change, and so God used this opportunity to grow in me a new trust in Him. He kept reminding me during this season that He alone is sufficient and that He would meet all of my needs. I really had to hang on to Him because I was without those close relationships with my girlfriends.**
>
> —Lindsey

Seasons of Life

The season you are experiencing in friendship is also likely to be influenced by the season of life that you are in. Each season has its unique demands, unique joys, and unique friendship opportunities. For example, if you have very young children, you might be surprised to know that there is more built-in relationship time during this season of motherhood than at most other times in life. You can call a friend and take the kids to the park and visit while they play. You can have your children nap at the same time so you can visit. I have put together a short list of seasons, and I encourage you to take advantage of the unique aspect of the season you are in and to see the importance of investing in these friendships as you look to the future.

Lessons From "The Greats"

Establish Friendship Traditions

Whether it's a monthly game of cards with a few couples, a "supper club" where you meet once a month and make dinner together, a day of the week to walk or play tennis, an annual Christmas cookie exchange, or even a family vacation together, create a tradition and commit to it.

I have personally witnessed (and experienced) the power of establishing friendship traditions. "The Greats" have been playing cards together once a month for over thirty years, they have taken a family vacation together for over twenty years, and they've walked together (Monday through Friday) for many years as well. "The Greats" attribute much of their ability to stay connected for so long to this single act of establishing a tradition and seeing it through.

Early Career

This time in life is usually marked by a high amount of freedom and a low amount of disposable income. I made my major turn down rebellion lane during this season and in retrospect think that getting connected with a core group of peers who were also believers would have been a tremendous source of encouragement and would have helped me forego much of the pain I went through because of poor choices.

One thing that was helpful for me was to spend time with couples who were grounded in their faith and could show me with their lives what is possible when you are committed to one another and to God.

Connecting Ideas for Growing Friendships During Early Career

- Seek out a mentor or mentors (spiritual, career).
- Form college/career groups at church.
- Make dinner with friends and then play some board games.
- Go to plays, shows, movies, concerts, local festivals/fairs.
- Travel.
- Take an exercise class together and then go out for a healthy bite to eat.
- Get outside on the weekends and do things (hike, kayak, bike, surf) that might be a little more challenging to do later in life should you start a family.

> **For women who are not married until later in life or not at all—it is very important to have close male friends. You can get the "guy stuff" even if you're not in a relationship. And you have guys to call when you need a date for an event. They are also good to talk to about guys you are dating and can give different feedback than you will get from your female friends. Plus, my guy friendships were generally easier to maintain and more relaxed. You miss their birthday? Oh well! You remember? and bring food? YAY for you! It was a good balance to the more intimate friendships with my girlfriends.**
>
> —Lorna

Early Motherhood

Let me be a model of hope to you. It was during this season that God threw me my lifeline in the form of friendship. So while there is a great possibility that you can feel isolated and lonely during the season of changing diapers, visiting the pediatrician countless times a week, and never getting to take a shower, there is ALSO the possibility of finding and growing awesome and amazing friendships. It can be done—I speak from experience. You might have to get a little creative and be flexible (I was queen of scheduling my children's naps and soon found out I needed to chill a little and let them sleep in the Pack 'n Play instead of their crib on occasion), but it can be done.

Connecting Ideas for Growing Friendships During Early Motherhood

- Set up play dates for your children; the likelihood of having a long conversation with your friend is not high, but at least you are together and you are getting a few sentences in here and there between watching the kids.

- When your husband is out of town, plan in advance to be with friends at those special hours between four and seven so that your children are still alive when your husband comes back! Give the kids baths together and let them wear each other out so when you go home or your friends leave, the kids will go right down and you can sit on the couch and watch a show, read a magazine, or go to bed yourself!

- Take advantage of the telephone and talk to a friend while you are getting the house picked up or while the kids are napping. Some of my favorite conversations happened while my friend Sue vacuumed and I did the dishes.

- Hire one baby-sitter for your children and your friend's children and go catch a matinee.

- Hit the following locations *together*:

  Beach

  Zoo

  Children's museum

  Park

  Mall

"You probably can have it all," Anna Quindlen muses. **"Just not all at the same time. And . . . you might have to make certain compromises when your children are**

small. But your children are going to be small for a very short period of time. It will go by in the blink of an eye, and you will only be 40, 50, 60 with another 15 or 25 years ahead of you."[6]

School-Aged Children

This is the season I am currently in, and I have learned two unchangeable truths:

- Other than your family, the people you spend the most time with are the ones sitting next to you at whatever extracurricular activity your children are involved in (sports team/drama club/dance).

- Other than your home, the place you will spend the most time is in your car as you shuttle your kids to and from school and events and activities.

One of the good things about this season of life is the opportunity to befriend women whom you might never have otherwise met. Such was the case for me the first year my son played flag football. The moms on that team bonded and decided to continue meeting every other month. Whenever we go out together, we get funny looks and sideways glances. It's as if people are scratching their heads and asking themselves, "How on earth did this group of women become friends?" Short, tall, loud, quiet, obsessive, compliant, easygoing, high-strung—we are an eclectic group, that is for sure. Yet we enjoy one another immensely and we all feel grateful that the Lord brought us together during one football season so that we can walk through the rest of the seasons of life together—even if we only get together a handful of times a year.

Connecting Ideas for Growing Friendships With School-Aged Children

Take Advantage of Modern Technology

Let's take a moment to thank God for cell phones, e-mail, and text messaging! Imagine, a decade ago mothers were held captive in their "taxis" and didn't have the ability to communicate with anybody over the age of ten! Can't you just feel the gratitude well up in your heart? Put your girlfriends on your speed dial so that when you need to distract yourself from the backseat bickering you need only press a button.

> **Could Alexander Graham Bell ever have imagined that he would one day become the patron saint of women's friendships?**[7]

Be Proactive

Schedule "friend time" in advance. With all the running around you will now be doing, you will definitely need to get your calendars in sync so you can get some time together. It's unlikely to just happen the way it might have when the kids were toddlers. Call your friend and pencil it in; catch a lunch here and there, do errands together while the kids are at school, walk and talk, do a Bible study together, or join a Moms In Touch prayer group at your children's school.[8]

Friendship in the Workforce

Try not to overlook the women that you spend a large portion of your day with. They may appear to be just co-workers, but the Lord may have other plans in mind like He did for my sister Katie:

> **Those girls had no idea what they were getting into. In one evening I had successfully roped Marnie, Lauren, and Abbi into helping me produce the Tour de Nez Pro Bike Race. The event was one month away and there was a year's worth of work still to be done. For the next month we worked both tirelessly and exhaustedly**

**alongside one another. We laughed hysterically when we
should have been crying, and we cried with each other
when others would have been laughing. Together we
both problem-solved and created new problems. We
threw our hands up together in moments of frustration
and threw our arms around one another in embraces of
gratitude and excitement. In one month we went from
casual acquaintances to best girlfriends, and we pulled
off an unforgettable event. We thought it was just a bike
race we were producing. It turned out
that we were giving birth to a lifelong friendship.**

Connecting Ideas for Growing Friendships in the Workforce

Multitask

Think through all that needs to get done and see if you can combine it with time with a girlfriend: working out at the gym, catching up on the phone while driving to and/or from work, shopping (grocery, Christmas, clothes), running errands, or pre-making dinners for the freezer together.

At Work

Have lunch with a co-worker, do a book study during lunch once a week, or see if one of your stay-at-home friends can meet you at work for lunch.

Here's some advice from the author of thirty-three books, including *Divine Stories of the Yahweh Sisterhood*, Michelle Medlock Adams:

It's a balancing act . . . you simply have to make time for friends because work will always rob you of your time if you let it. I always have an article deadline looming or a book manuscript that is due or an interview to prepare for, or a writer's conference to attend, and those are important to my writing and speaking career. But if I let those eat up all of my time and neglect my friends, those friendships will wither.

I've often heard that children spell love T-I-M-E, and do you know what? I think friends spell love the same way. So schedule a pedicure together, or meet at the track and walk and talk, or plan a "play date" for the kiddos and catch up at the park. Just pencil it in on your planner and stick to it as if it were an important deadline, because it is important. My advice? Don't let your career dictate your life. If you do, your relationship with the Lord will suffer, your marriage will suffer, your children will suffer, and your friends will suffer. Carve out time for the important people in your life, and plan ahead. Careers and kids make spur-of-the-moment outings a bit of a challenge, so plan a dessert date and write it down on your planner. Then look forward to it and don't cancel it unless you have an emergency. Go, eat chocolate, catch up with your friends, and enjoy! View your friends as gifts from God because that's exactly what they are.

Preteen/Teen Years

My girlfriend Nancy has two teenage daughters and told me that in this season of life, it is imperative that you have friends, especially women whose children are the same age as yours. She explained that at this stage, the kids desire more independence; they don't come to talk to you as much as they used to, but you still need to be available for them. Here's a little more input from Nancy:

As I find myself getting older, especially during the season of parenting teenagers, the relationships with my girlfriends and even connections with women in general (from Bible study groups to movie nights) have become more than valuable; *they are vital*. These relationships add sweetness to my life. They remind me I am more than a mom. They remind me I am a woman who is a friend, who can laugh and play, cry, care, and be cared for. This keeps me from waiting around for the day when my children "arise and call me blessed" (Proverbs 31:28). I say this jokingly now, even though it is possible to become so focused on parenting and desiring

affirmations for my efforts that I lose sight of the big picture and neglect other aspects of who I have been created to be.

Vacation Together

Schedule your spring and/or summer vacations with other families with teenagers. You get to stay connected and keep an eye on the kids at the same time. This is one of the reasons we recently purchased a boat. We realized that we only have a few more years of our children wanting to be with us, but if we have the boat, even when we're un-cool they'll want to invite their friends to go boating. We'll not only be able to enjoy them, but keep a pulse on their relationships with their peers. This is also what motivated our in-laws to build a pool—so theirs could be the house that the kids' friends want to come over to. Camping, hiking, and day trips to the lake or ocean together are less-expensive vacation ideas that offer the same opportunity for the whole family to be with their friends.

Sandwich Generation

The sandwich generation is loosely defined as people who are taking care of their children and their ailing parents at the same time. I am in a bit of an unusual situation because of the close relationship (and geographical proximity) that I've had with my grandparents over the years. As a result, I am experiencing some of the unique stresses of this season. I am trying to get my kids to all the events they need to be at, help them with their homework, take care of the daily household demands, be a wife who is available and engaged, meet my deadline for this book, and take the time to visit and care for my grandma, who has recently been placed in hospice care. There are days when I know for a fact that I need a "friend fuel-up lunch" because I am running on empty, and then when I am in the process of enjoying my friend's company, I feel a pang of guilt because I *should* be spending more time with my grandma. It's a daily battle!

For many weeks I've been grappling with God—complaining, crying, whining, and fighting because I don't understand why the timing is such that I am writing this book while I am saying good-bye to the woman who has been like a mother to me. Just last night (while I was crying in the shower) it dawned on me that this book is not a burden but a gift. A gift the Lord is giving me to help me through this time of letting go of the woman who encouraged, nurtured, and prayed for me. Through writing this book I am being reminded of the women in my life. These friends are helping me through this difficult time, and they are the ones who will continue to nurture, love, and support me long after my grandma is gone.

In fact, just the other day my friend Andrea called, and I told her that I was having a hard time getting off the couch or even out of my pajamas because I was so sad about Grandma. Andrea said to me, "Get up and get a hot washcloth. Think about how good it's going to feel to wash your face. Then I want you to get dressed and get on with life for today. Tracy, this sadness won't be fixed by having one or two 'down days.' We know that because you've already had a few, so today let's get your face washed, get you dressed, and get you going. You've got to get the kids picked up from school and get out to see your grandma, so let's go." Now, I have to say, these words didn't make me feel any better, but they were true and necessary nonetheless.

This sandwich generation season has been a valuable reminder for me to continue to invest in my friendships (even if it's just with check-in phone calls here and there because that's all that time permits) and to see that they are God's way of providing me with feminine nurturing, care, and encouragement.

Empty Nest and Beyond . . .

Each of my closest friends are what I like to refer to as my "heart" friends. They have claimed a piece of my heart because of their love for me with the gift of their friendship. When it comes to my friendships now that my nest is empty, I find that I have more quality time to give to the friendship without the mom distractions. I tune in,

**and the friendship has the possibility of
moving into a deeper, more meaningful level.**

—Sheri Torelli, author and speaker

As you are now aware, "The Greats" are some of my favorite empty-nesters, so I approached them about the subject of friendship during this season of life. They informed me that in the years after the kids left home, in addition to playing cards together once a month and vacationing together, they've also begun to do things together like eat dinner as a group once a week (they meet at a different restaurant every Monday), exercise together, play golf together, and travel together. Once traveling came up, these ladies looked at one another and said, "Remember China?" and with misty eyes they recounted one of their most memorable trips.

For years Stan Long had wanted to see the Great Wall of China, so four couples (from the larger group of "The Greats") made plans to do a tour through Asia. The friends made their way through Seoul, Bangkok, Singapore, Hong Kong, and Japan. As the trip progressed, Stan could tell that his health was deteriorating (prone to pneumonia because of his chronic obstructive pulmonary disease [COPD], he was having difficulty breathing), but he kept this to himself so as not to affect his friends and their trip. He took to staying on the tour bus when he got tired and encouraging his friends to go ahead without him. By the time the group arrived in China, Stan needed to use the hotel wheelchair to make it around. The friends arrived at the proximity of the Wall, and Jean began to push her husband, Stan, in his wheelchair up the steep incline. When the group had about six blocks to go, the unthinkable happened. One of the wheels on Stan's chair broke, and the chair refused to budge. To Stan's dismay, it appeared as though his dream would not be realized; however, what Stan had not taken into account was the determination of his friends to make his dream a reality. Immediately upon realizing the situation, Stan's friends surrounded him. One of the men tipped the chair back so that it rested on its two steady wheels, while the other two men grabbed hold of either side of the chair. Slowly and steadily the group made their way over the rough and rocky terrain to get their friend Stan to the Great Wall. When one of the men would tire, they would switch spots until they had each been a part of helping Stan realize his dream. Jean would later write in her journal, *"What great friends we have!"*

Lessons From "The Greats"

Do not put off traveling until you all retire. Do it when you can because you never know what the future holds.

Connecting Ideas for Growing Friendships During the Empty-Nest Years

- Eat meals together regularly (restaurants or at home).
- Exercise together (walking, biking, fitness center).
- Travel together.
- Teach (a class, a craft, a Bible study).
- Volunteer with a friend for a cause that you both feel strongly about.
- Celebrate your children's milestones (births, birthdays, graduations, weddings) together.
- Mentor and befriend younger women.

My friends share my faith—we encourage each other in our walks with the Lord. One friend is about fifteen years older than I am—her life experience and her faithfulness to our God have carried me through some difficult times. She is a good listener and her advice is always worth consideration.

—Lorna

 **Ponder**

Have you ever had a friendship take on a new shape? How did it change?

How challenging is it for you to remain flexible with your friendships?

What season of friendship are you currently in?

Describe a time in your life when you experienced a season of narrowing.

Did you find yourself stuck anywhere in this chapter? Did you find a place that needs the healing touch of God or the strength and courage to move forward?

 Pray

Father God, thank you for the season I am currently in. I confess that I can feel resentful of this season because _____ (list feelings and reasons here), *but I know that you have a plan and a purpose for me while I am here and I don't want to miss it. Open my eyes to the unique friendship opportunities that I have, help me be a good steward of the relationships that I'm currently in, and cause me to be bold in reaching out to the new people you place in my life. In Jesus' name, amen.*

 **Apply**

Start the ball rolling on the one idea that sounded appealing to you from this chapter. If it was vacationing together, then call some friends to initiate that first conversation. If it was taking a trip to the zoo with another family, get that on the calendar.

Chapter 11

Losing Blossoms From Your Crown

*Sometimes when certain names come up it still hurts . . .
it still feels so painful.*

—Anonymous

You will grieve, but your grief will turn to joy.

John 16:20

There are times when blossoms fall from the crowns we wear and other times when new blossoms are woven in.

A move, a disagreement, a change in schools, churches, activities, even death . . . there are many reasons why a daisy might leave our crown, leave our inner circle. I like to think of these situations as *daisies that have moved from the crown we wear to a bouquet we see* when we walk into the rooms of our memories. If a betrayal or a deep wound is the cause of a loss, such a light description might sound inappropriate. When you feel that a blossom has not merely fallen from your crown but been ripped away, it often feels less painful to think of that person as out of your life, gone for good, or in the case of death, stolen from your life.

If this is indeed what you are feeling, I would like you to consider something: Even though your friend is no longer in your life, does it take away the gift that she was or the gifts that she gave you through her presence at the time you were close? Does her absence now negate the blessings, the laughter, the joy, the comfort that she brought you during the season you were together?

Even though there have been daisies in my life that have moved from my crown to a bouquet through very challenging and extremely painful circumstances, it *does not* take away the gift or impact that these friends had *at the time when we were together*. It does not lessen the blessing they were or the lessons that I learned, and I would not change the role they had in my life or discount the gift of their friendship simply because we are not as close on this day due to geography, difficulty, or even death. They are still in my life, just not in the same way they used to be. However, because our hearts were knit together, because our stems and our lives were woven together, there is pain, there is loss, and there is emptiness in the place where they once were.

Think back to that daisy chain. If you take a daisy out of the crown, there is an empty spot, a hole in the crown, an empty slit in the stem. When a friendship ends or goes through a period of reshaping, pain is inevitable.

There are four actions that have been of great help when I am going through a season of transition in a friendship.

Praying Specifically

One thing that has been helpful for me as I journey through seasons such as these is praying specifically for my friend. I know from personal experience that praying for your friend is the last thing you want to do when you are feeling hurt or betrayed, but it is a way I have found that I can continue to love my friends (which God calls me to do) in the midst of feeling hurt by them.

One way to do this is by choosing a symbol (a visual "prayer starter") that will remind you to pray for the friend that you are estranged from or feeling awkwardness toward. It could be a picture of her, a gift that she gave you, an old card that she sent that you can now use as a bookmark, or in my case a mug that you drink your daily cup of tea or coffee from. . . . Whatever it is, use it as a reminder to love her with prayer. In my first book, *Prayer Starters for Busy Moms*, I write about such a time:

> **As I placed that mug on the shelf, I uttered a prayer of blessing over my friend, and while my true desire was to push that mug to the back of the shelf (as I desired to push the pain to the back of my mind), the Lord had me**

**place that mug front and center so that
I could pray each day as I opened the cupboard.**[1]

Remaining Flexible in the Hands of the Gardener

As I mentioned at the beginning of the book, the lifeline of friends that came into my life and changed everything for me occurred when my children were infants. My friends and I really lived life together, and while we didn't take for granted our special bond, I don't think any of us realized that the quantity of time we got to spend together during this season of our lives was unique. Once all of our children started school (in different neighborhoods) and began to get involved in (different) sports and activities, the amount of time we got to spend together diminished drastically. Times changed, circumstances changed . . . we were now the carpool moms who were running to fourteen different meetings, practices, and errands. I experienced growing pains in these friendships because I missed seeing my friends on a daily basis and I missed the ease with which our friendships took place. I was also aware that this was just the way it was. It wasn't that any of my friends had done anything to me, that we had gotten in a giant fight, or that we had decided we needed mutual space from the relationship. Our friendships were changing because circumstances were changing. No matter how much I resisted this change, it was taking place. I'm still learning that remaining flexible in God's hands and allowing my friendships to take on the shape He wants them to take allows me to experience more peace in the process.

There are other times, however, when the changes in your friendship may not seem simply circumstantial. This morning when I was spending time in the Word, I came to this verse from the book of Amos: "Do two people walk hand in hand if they aren't going to the same place?" (3:3 THE MESSAGE). It made me think of the ambivalence I've felt of late in a few friendships.

My husband and I have been working (and praying and ministering) alongside many people for over a decade to establish a church and school in a growing community in Southern California. In partnering toward this common cause, many friendships have bloomed and grown; however, there have also been friends over the years who have moved on to different churches and to different schools. Those relational relocations have left me at times feeling hurt, angry, betrayed, lonely, and deeply sad. A recurring thought I've had regarding these friends is, "Wait a minute, I thought we were in this together . . . I thought we were battling together, building together, pushing back the forces of darkness together, and partnering with Christ to establish His church and His school together." Months pass and I haven't known quite what to do with these friendships and the growing ambivalence I feel.

In rereading C. S. Lewis's *The Four Loves*, I was once again comforted by his teaching that "friendship must be *about* something"[2] (emphasis mine). Lewis's teaching has helped me to make some sense of my feelings of ambivalence . . . he's helped me to understand that my friendships used to be about building a church and a school together, but since we no longer have that common bond, the friendship needs to be redefined . . . to become *about* something else. I don't have to make my friend's decision to leave a "bad choice" and my decision to stay a "good choice" (and I certainly pray that all my friend(s) choose not to do the same thing). I've realized that the fact that I don't know where to go from here is okay, and actually to be expected. I can choose to rely on God and His perfect timing to lead me and to lead my friends. I can choose to remain as flexible as clay in the hand of the Potter, or for the purposes of this book, as flexible as a daisy in the hands of the Master Gardener. I will allow God to take these blossoms and place them in a different bouquet in my life or even in the garden of my memories. You can do the same thing too, if you choose.

Choosing Gratitude

I am glad for my girlfriends, even the ones who are no longer a part of my life. I treasure the memories and

**what I learned from each of them. I hope they
know in their own hearts what they meant to me.**

—Sheri Torelli, author and speaker

To get to the place I described earlier in this chapter, where you feel grateful for the blessing that your fallen blossom has been in your life, is truly a movement of God's grace. One of the ways I believe you can work with God to help create an environment for this grace to manifest itself is by dwelling on the things you are grateful for about your friend. To do this, take out a sheet of paper and write your friend's name at the top. Then start writing down anything and everything you can think of that you are grateful for about her:

- She made me feel welcome when we moved to the neighborhood.
- She came to my side when my mom died.
- She loved my kids with her time and her talents.
- She has a great laugh and we laughed a lot together.
- She always made the best chocolate chip cookies.
- She never forgot my birthday.
- She was instrumental in my walk with the Lord.
- She prayed for me, and I know she still does.

Looking Ahead

**A friend and I recently reconnected after a time away,
and it is great. We understand each other more. Sometimes you have to step away for a season.**

—Nancy H.

God's ways are higher than my ways; His understanding is greater than mine. I always need to come back to the fact that God is the source of all wisdom, and while I may not understand what He is doing, I can put my trust in Him. While it may sound cliché, "I don't know what the future holds, but I know who holds my future—and my friends' as well," and so I can choose to hope.

One of the original subtitle options for this book was "Planting and Cultivating LIFELONG Relationships." To be honest, I had initial concerns with the word *lifelong* in the title because it seemed loaded and didn't communicate that there might be times when God calls us to take *time away* from a certain friendship. That being said, I do believe that friends who share the common bond of Christ are always involved in lifelong relationships, for eventually we *will* share eternity together.

My dear friend Gina reminisces about one of her fallen blossoms:

> Daisy chains remind me of my high school days back in the '70s when I wore daisy chains in my hair. (I was quite the hippy!) The thing that made daisies so appealing was their simplicity—they could be found anywhere, along a roadside or in a field, and they almost looked like they were smiling. . . . Just mentioning Cathy and our friendship brings tears to my eyes. We had a deep friendship—I would liken it to a sixth sense. It's been about fifteen years since she died, a very long time, but I remember her like I saw her yesterday.
>
> In retrospect, it was a very short friendship, but for five or six years we had a friendship that books are written about: a deep, soul-filled love for each other. It was an unlikely friendship too. She came from an educated family—polished, so to speak—while I, in contrast, came from the other side of the tracks. I think it was the classic "opposites attract."
>
> But, like daisies, our friendship was simple. We accepted each other as we were—absent of expectations. There was no need for therapy; we were each other's therapist. Our equal desire to know and love our Lord Jesus and everything that embodies a Christ-filled life was enough. It was a wonderful season, so full of hope. My fondest memory of our friendship comes from a fall women's retreat. We brought girly stuff to

do manicures. Cathy had never had a pedicure—I had only had one or two myself. (Women didn't really do that back in the '80s.) We stayed up all night, and I washed her feet, trimmed her toenails, and polished her tootsies. We laughed while I was washing her feet, commenting on how gross her heels were and how I was a nut for cleaning them. We had a blast and talked about it for months. The following spring Cathy was diagnosed with non-Hodgkin's lymphoma. A season of grief replaced our season of simplicity, and eighteen months later Cathy died.

When I reflect on the days we spent comparing parenting tips, how to love and honor our husbands, and exchanging recipes, my favorite memory is of when I washed her feet. How privileged I am to have honored my friend, my sister in Christ, and joyfully washed her feet. Everyone should have a friend, even if only for a season, whose feet they would find joy in washing.

Though life is not as simple as it was (or maybe it is but the seasons of life have given me thicker skin), I still have hope. Because I know we share the same faith, I have hope that I will see Cathy again. I look forward to her smile and her quiet spirit, and I know that when we finally make it to eternity, it won't be just for a season.

Lessons From "The Greats"

Enjoy the Season

Don't put off enjoying your life by believing that next year life will be easier. This is a setup for discontent. Life keeps on going, and often it doesn't get easier; it changes, and you will have regrets that you didn't enjoy what you had while you had it.

In telling one of my wisest friends about "The Greats," he remarked, "By living each day to the fullest with one another, and by getting the most out of each day, 'The Greats' reduce the inevitable loss that we all eventually feel."[3]

 ## Ponder

Who are the blossoms that have fallen from your crown?

After reading this chapter, which exercise ("Praying Specifically," "Remaining Flexible," "Choosing Gratitude," "Looking Ahead") do you feel will be most beneficial in helping you view your "fallen blossom" friends as still in your life but perhaps in a different way than before?

Did you find yourself stuck anywhere in this chapter? Did you find a place that needs the healing touch of God or the strength and courage to move forward?

 ## Pray

There is a time for everything, and a season for every activity under heaven. He has made everything beautiful in its time.

(Ecclesiastes 3:1, 11)

Father God, I thank you for this promise that you make "everything beautiful in its time." Right now I am going through a season of _____ (confess your thoughts here) *and I feel* _____ (confess your feelings here). *Help me to embrace the season I am in right now. Don't let me miss anything about it. I want to be fully present and I want to be available to be used by you. I thank you that I don't have to rely on my own wisdom and understanding, but that I can put my hope in you. I thank you that the relationships I invest in here on earth are lifelong because I know we will spend eternity together worshiping you.*

Apply

Choose a visual prayer starter for a blossom who has fallen from your daisy crown so that you are reminded to pray for her.

Place the name of a friend who has fallen from your crown at the top of a page. Write down at least ten things you can thank the Lord for that your friend brought into your life. (For example: She always made me laugh; she was there for me when my husband was sick; she introduced me to sushi.)

Letters From a Friend

Dear Friend,

I know deep within my soul I have found a true friend, and that when I fall you will always be there for me. Your friendship to me is a glimpse of God.

I love you,
Michele

Chapter 12

An Invitation Into the Garden

Reach out to the world with the light and love of Christ.

In order to thrive, we must stay in the presence of the
Son, in the soil of His Word, and receive the continual
washing, cleansing rain of His Holy Spirit. As we do this,
we will look around and see that we are surrounded by
other daisies, ready to be called by the Father for His
purposes, ready to be invited
to be the "light of the world."

(See Matthew 5:14.)

Each friend represents a world in us, a world
possibly not born until they arrive.[1]

—Anaïs Nin

She stood, hand poised to knock on the door. *What am I doing?* Kay
thought to herself for what seemed like the hundredth time. Invited
to attend a neighborhood Bible study just two doors down from her
own house, Kay was a nervous wreck. Eight years of secretly suffering with agoraphobia had kept her housebound, and finally, with the
comfort of being close enough to home to escape if necessary, Kay was
venturing out. *It's only two doors down,* she'd consoled herself earlier in
the week. Now as she stood at the door she told herself, *Just take the
seat closest to the door and you'll be okay.* Kay finally knocked, the door
opened, and a friendly voice called, "Come on over."

To Kay's surprise, the voice came from a woman in a hospital bed
set up in the middle of the living room. With a beautiful smile and a
surprising calmness, Leslie, the hostess of the study, motioned to one
of the chairs that encircled her bed. Kay soon learned that this young
mother had terminal cancer. The disease, however, had not robbed

Leslie of her zeal for Christ or her desire to reach out to the women in her neighborhood. Leslie led the women through a study called "Friendship Bible Coffee" that day, and Kay sat quietly the whole hour without saying a word. To Kay's relief, nobody made her feel awkward regarding her lack of participation, and before she knew it, it was time to go home. Week after week Kay looked forward to her "outings" to Leslie's house. She was particularly inspired by the peace and ease Leslie exhibited, given her illness and all that she would soon leave behind.

Before long Kay discovered that this group of women also attended a monthly luncheon. It would be a huge step for Kay to go as it would require being farther away from the security of her home. (Leslie used to attend as well but could no longer do so.) After much fretting, Kay finally decided to go, but when the day of the luncheon arrived, the friend who was going to take her there got sick. Kay, determined to attend but knowing she couldn't go alone, called her sister and begged her to pick her up and go to the luncheon with her. Her sister consented, and that day Kay met even more wonderful women who would soon become part of a much needed lifeline of friendship.

Kay has now been involved with Stonecroft Ministries for more than thirty years. I met her when I spoke to her group. This former agoraphobic has served in many capacities, leading "Friendship Bible Coffees" (recently renamed "Stonecroft Bible Studies"), speaking at luncheons, chairing events, and organizing conferences. Kay still credits that *initial invitation* as the turning point in her life. "The women there became my family. . . . They were there for me and they came through for me!" All because *one woman* opened her home and reached out to a potential friend with the life-changing love of Christ.

Have you ever extended an invitation to someone? Given them the opportunity to "come and see"? It doesn't have to be a group that you are personally leading or a class that you are personally teaching; perhaps it is simply an invitation to attend church with you on Easter or Christmas, or to go away for a girls' weekend, a conference, or a retreat.

For more than a decade now, I have been attending my church's fall women's retreat. It is the tradition at these retreats for the women to take some time before heading down the mountain and back to their everyday lives, to share with the other women what God did for them over the course of the weekend. It is always a profound and intimate time of heartfelt sharing. Year after year I've been a part of this circle, and year after year I've heard a common theme:

**I am so thankful to God for all of you women;
I don't know what I would do without you.**

**I've been trying to do life on my own. Now I see that I
don't need to do that anymore. I need Christ;
He loves me, and all of you helped me see that.**

I was lonely, but now I've been invited into this circle.

One of the most amazing privileges we have as children of God is the ministry of reconciliation. We read in 2 Corinthians 5:18, 20: "And all of this is a gift from God, who brought us back to himself through Christ. And God has given us this task of reconciling people to him. So we are Christ's ambassadors; God is making his appeal through us. We speak for Christ when we plead, 'Come back to God!'" (NLT).

We don't have to have the gift of evangelism or have a degree in theology to help people *see* Jesus. One of the best ways to show people that they have a friend in Jesus is by being a friend to them, by offering up your life to them in love.

Once I came to know Christ as my personal Savior I felt a desire to do "big things for God," to really make His name known throughout the earth. (I tend to be slightly dramatic with a tendency toward all-or-nothing compulsiveness—can you tell?) I soon became aware that Christ was not calling me to "do big things," but to be faithful with the little things and to love the people He was placing in my midst on a daily basis.

At the time, I was teaching aerobics several times a week. So before I went to each class, I began to pray that the Lord would fill me to overflowing with His Holy Spirit and that He would use me to love and encourage the women in my class. I prayed that God would show me the woman who needed a hug or a word of encouragement, and that He would tell me what songs to play that would inspire and pour His Truth into their lives. I asked Him to shine His light through me as I went about the day so that Christ would draw each one to himself. An extremely powerful and freeing verse is found in the book of John: "But I, when I am lifted up from the earth, will draw all men to myself" (12:32). Isn't it awesome to know that we don't have to feel pressure to make people believe? We don't even possess that power. We simply need to lift up Christ with our lives, and He will draw them to himself.

You don't have to be on a platform speaking to thousands to have an effect on the kingdom of God. All you need is a willing heart and a life that is ready to be used. Whether you are among others at your place of work, standing in line at the grocery store, or reading your children a bedtime story, God can use you to invite people to know His Son Jesus Christ.

Opening Your Home and Heart

Friendships, like geraniums, bloom in kitchens.[2]

—Blanche H. Geffant

A few years into my walk with the Lord I felt a nudging to open my home and host my first book study (*The Path* by Laurie Beth Jones). Whenever I felt this nudging I would shove it back down. I was intimidated by the thought of leading a small group. I felt anxious that I wouldn't know what I was doing (give me a stage and a large group of women any day over the intimacy of a small number of ladies staring at me). Nevertheless, for many months I wrestled with this nudging. As I prayed it through one day, the Lord put a few specific women on my heart, so I made a deal with Him. (I know you must be amazed at my spiritual maturity!) I said, "Okay, I'll talk to Sarah (one of the women who had been on my heart), and if she's interested in being in a small group with me, I'll do it." (I was hoping beyond hope that she would say, "Thanks, but no thanks.") A few days later I was with my friend Sarah and her kids at the park. As we were leaving I turned to her and said, "Sarah, if I were to do a book study, I mean, like, I don't even know if I will, but say I did; I mean, if I *were* to have a study at my house, is that something you'd want to be a part of?" Before I could finish stammering out what I was trying to say, Sarah responded, "Anytime, anywhere, any day that you do it, I will be there." I walked back to the car shaking my head. Isn't that just like God? You open the door slightly, and He lets you know exactly what He wants you to do!

I sent out personal invitations to the twelve women that the Lord had placed on my heart. I let them know we were going to meet once a week for nine weeks through the summer. Most of them said yes, and so began an AMAZING time of connection and ministry. Week after week I prepared my home (i.e., loaded the dishwasher, got the kids to the baby-sitter, and if there was time, lit a candle), the women showed up, and the Holy Spirit led our time together. It was beautiful, intimate—truly one of the best times in my life, because I was relying completely on the Lord's strength and guidance rather than my own, and He was showing me how He wanted to work through me and through the women that sat next to me. Women came to Christ through that time, women were baptized, and women were made aware of the power of relationship and how God wants to work through relationships. I learned that when I open my home and open my heart, I will be a blessing and be blessed in the process. I learned that I don't need to know how to do it (whatever "it" happens to be), I simply need to reach out to the women that God is calling me to reach out to.

To watch a woman choose to receive Christ as her personal Savior, to hold her hand and listen to her cry out to her heavenly Father, to see her transformed into a new creation right before your eyes . . . is nothing less than an awesome privilege. I always shake my head in pure amazement when moments like these happen—moments when

I am made aware that God used a woman with feet of clay to pull another woman into the garden and back into the fold.

That summer study became a tradition. The following year I encouraged the original gals to personally invite a few women that the Lord had placed on their hearts. We were bursting the seams of my house that summer, so much so that the following summer we met at our church and over fifty women attended. Two of the women from the original small group gave me a plaque that hangs in my kitchen—the symbolic garden in my life. It says:

Welcome to My Garden, Dahhling!

Will you let God use you too? Will you allow the Holy Spirit to use you to invite women into the garden of God's grace? If you are willing to open your heart, you never know how or when God will use you to draw another woman back into His arms.

One of my favorite old hymns is "Come, Thou Fount of Every Blessing."[3] One line reads, "Jesus sought me when a stranger, wandering from the fold of God." Jesus might use you to seek out one of His lost ones. He might use you like He used Leslie to invite a wandering woman like Kay into the fold, into the garden, back to her rightful place within the loving embrace of family.

Lessons From "The Greats"

The Invitation to Journey Together

> For the past twenty-five years we've been walking together. Five days a week you can see us out there. We always walk at the same time, and we always walk the same route (that loops around the neighborhood). People have asked us why we don't take a different route. "Don't you get bored?" they say. But we've never changed our walking route because we've always wanted people to know that they are welcome to join us. Sometimes there have been women who have been caught up with life and missed months of walking at a

time, and we want them to know they are still welcome
to join us. Other times a gal may have gotten up late and
missed the beginning of the walk—well, she can count
on the fact that pretty soon we will loop back around
and she can join us then. No, we won't vary our walking
route. The most important part about our group is for
people to know that whatever season they are in, however many days they may have missed, they are always
invited to join in and journey with us.

Resources

If you would like to host a Bible study for "seekers," I highly recommend Stonecroft Ministries. The studies are easy to follow, easy
to lead, and the materials are priced reasonably (e-mail: *biblestudies@
stonecroft.org*).

If you are more interested in mentoring or you want a more in-
depth resource for discipling new believers one-on-one, the book
Personal Disciple Making by Christopher B. Adsit is a wonderful choice
(published by Campus Crusade for Christ).

Some terrific books that have easy-to-follow group study materials
include:

Wired That Way by Marita and Florence Littauer

Captivating by John and Stasi Eldredge

Keeping a Princess Heart in a Not-So-Fairy-Tale World by Nicole
Johnson

The Path by Laurie Beth Jones

Boundaries by John Cloud and Henry Townsend

 ## Ponder

Who did God use to invite you into the garden?

What feelings come up when you think about reaching out to women
in this way?

Did you find yourself stuck anywhere in this chapter? Did you find a place that needs the healing touch of God or the strength and courage to move forward?

 ## Pray

Lord, is there a woman in my life or a family that you are calling me to reach out to? I confess that sometimes I feel (scared, intimidated, freaked out, anxious) when I think about telling people about your love. Give me courage, Lord, and help me to remember that all I need to do is be myself and to communicate with my life and with my words what has happened ever since I asked you into my heart.

Please show me what you want me to do—if it is inviting this person to dinner, to church, or to coffee. I need you to lead the way. I also ask that you would prepare their heart for friendship. In Jesus' name, amen.

 ## Apply

Write a letter to the woman (or man) who first invited you to experience the grace of Jesus. You might have more than one letter to write if there was more than one person (which is often the case). Tell them what it meant to you and how it has impacted your life.

Take out a piece of paper and make three vertical columns. In the first column write "Before Jesus," in the second, "Asking Jesus in," and in the third, "Since Jesus." Spend fifteen minutes and think through what your life was like before Christ came in, what made you aware of your need for Christ, and what has happened since Christ has become Lord of your life. This is your "witness," the way your life has changed since becoming a Christian, and this is a tool to help you let your new friends know what Jesus means to you.

If you attend a place of worship regularly, find out if there are any upcoming events that you could invite someone to (a retreat, a tea, a Bible study, MOPS).

Invite some friends over for a "spa night." Light a candle, pass a facial mask around, throw in a chick flick, and make sure you have some form of chocolate to serve.

Do you have a gift or talent such as knitting, photography, crocheting, cake decorating, or other fun craft or activity? Why not offer to teach someone else how to do this? My sister owns a restaurant, and she often teaches friends how to bake bread or pies. It's a great way for them to learn a new task and for her to share her love for them.

Closing Thoughts

Ladies, isn't it awesome that our lives are "full with girls"! Our lives are full of daisies just waiting to be made into chains and into crowns. Let us hold fast to friendship, to give to our friends and to receive from them all that God intends.

Psalm 103 says, "Praise the Lord, O my soul, and forget not all his benefits—who redeems your life from the pit and *crowns you* with love and compassion, who satisfies your desires with good things" (vv. 2, 4-5, emphasis mine).

I hope you can see that one of the ways our Lord "crowns us with love and compassion" is by encircling us with growing friendships and teaching us to encircle others in the same way. Blessings to you, my friend; I am trusting that "the Lord will guide you always...will satisfy your needs. . . . You will be like a well-watered garden, like a spring whose waters never fail" (Isaiah 58:11).

Keep your face to the sunshine and you cannot see the shadow. It's what sunflowers do.[4]

—Helen Keller

Appendix

Two Dozen Ways to Demonstrate Love and Devotion to the "Daisies in Your Chain"

1. Pray for the people in her life (husband, children, extended family).
2. Take chicken soup to her when she is sick, and then take her kids home with you so she can rest.
3. Save articles that she might be interested in reading.
4. Record her favorite show for her when you know she's going to miss it.
5. Make her a birthday gift that represents different aspects of her personality that you admire and enjoy (bright yellow wrapping paper because "she shines," a cross necklace because of her love for the Lord, a leopard print bow to represent her "wild side," and a funny card to hear that laugh you love).
6. Make her a basket of her favorite snacks when she is leaving on a trip.
7. Write her a prayer for each day of her trip and number the envelopes.
8. Put fresh milk, eggs, and bread in her kitchen, along with a big sign that says "Missed You!" to welcome her home from her trip.
9. Do a dinner exchange with her. (You cook enough for both of your families one night a week and she cooks on a different

night. You've given each other a home-cooked meal and a night off!)

10. Call her to say, "I was thinking of you!"
11. Ask her how she is doing and then give her your undivided attention.
12. Clean her house when crisis strikes.
13. Arrange to surprise her with a "Girlfriend Getaway."
14. Make arrangements for your friend (baby-sitter, the day off work) and steal her away for lunch and a matinee.
15. Remind her with your words, with Scripture, and with action that she is "loved with an everlasting love" (see Jeremiah 31:3) and that she is "the beloved" (see Song of Solomon).
16. Buy a CD of encouraging music to minister to her through a difficult season.
17. Write a letter on pretty stationery that affirms your commitment to the friendship when you are going through an awkward time with each other.
18. Show up for the special events in her life (births, dedications, baptisms, funerals, birthdays, other celebrations).
19. Bake or buy your friend's favorite dessert and place it on a pretty plate with a note that says, "You make life so sweet."
20. Leave a message on her voice mail: "This is what I am praying for you today . . ."
21. When making a casserole, double the recipe and drop it off "just because."
22. Celebrate her victories (and her family's victories) with her by "jumping and screaming" in your own special way.
23. Give her a hug every time you see her.
24. Tell her the truth with gentleness, forgive her for not being everything you need, and always point her in the direction of her very best friend—Jesus Christ.

**No one has ever seen God; but if we love one another,
God lives in us and his love is made complete in us.**

(1 John 4:12)

Acknowledgments

As iron sharpens iron, so one man sharpens another.

(Proverbs 27:17)

First of all, my heartfelt thanks go out to my husband for his continual outpouring of love, prayers, and support. Along with all that love he gave me my first *NIV Study Bible* . . . who knew that in doing so he would be starting a tradition of study that would be influential in ministering inside and outside of our home?!

At Bethany House I'd especially like to thank Kyle and Julie for continuing to believe that the Lord has put a pen in my hand for a reason. I also want to send out a big *Merci!* to my editor, Ellen, and a standing ovation to the graphics/design department . . . it is my humble opinion that Bethany House creates the most magnificent books in the business!

To the women who have taken the time out of their busy ministry schedules to not only read this book but to thoughtfully and beautifully back this book with their words and their reputations: Fern Nichols, Joni Eareckson Tada, Emilie Barnes, Nicole Johnson, and Michelle Medlock Adams. Thank you, I AM HONORED!

To "The Greats," aka "The Valencia Hills Moms" (especially Marion, Jean, and Carole), thank you for sharing your lives, your stories, and your wisdom.

To Kay Rust for sharing your testimony and the story of the woman who "invited you into the garden."

To my "Uprooted and Transplanted" ladies: Elizabeth, Jean, Patti, Dena, Mom, Lindsey, Tammy, Julie, and Lara. Your honest input was insightful and valuable.

To all those who offered valuable input and/or wonderful writing: Marita Littauer, Georgia Shaffer, Dena Dyer, Pepper and Nell

Sweeney, Cathy MacAdam, Gina Bogna, Sue White, Kathy Spencer, Lorna Bob, Gabbi Klein, Jennifer Kendall, Sheri Torelli, Andrea White, Shirley Almeida, Joanne and Gina, Nancy Stemme, Jayne Fall, my sisters Nancy Horn and Katie Louvat, and Allison Bottke (my Glorieta Angel).

And finally, to Julie Luepke, who showed us all what courage, love, hope, and faith look like.

Endnotes

Introduction

1. Dawson Trotman, quoted in Rick Warren, *The Purpose-Driven Life* (Grand Rapids, MI: Zondervan, 2002), 308.

Chapter 1

1. *The American Heritage® Dictionary of the English Language, 4ᵗʰ edition*, Houghton Mifflin Company. *www.answers.com/topic/daisy-chain*
2. *Webster's Ninth New Collegiate Dictionary* (Springfield, MA: Merriam-Webster, Inc., 1983), 493.
3. C.S. Lewis, *The Four Loves* (Orlando, FL: Harcourt, 1988), 57.
4. Ibid., 71.
5. Alice Hayes, "How to Daisy Chain," *www.flowerbud.com/flowerPress/daisy.asp*, 2/15/2004.

Chapter 2

1. Dr. David White, senior pastor, NorthPark Community Church.
2. Brenda Hunter and Holly Larson, *In the Company of Friends* (Sisters, OR: Multnomah/Questar, 1996), 26.
3. Corrie Cutrer, "Power of Two," *Today's Christian Woman* (July/August 2003): 36.

Chapter 3

1. Hunter and Larson, *In the Company of Friends*, 135.
2. Lewis, *The Four Loves*, 126.
3. Adapted from Brennan Manning, *Abba's Child* (Colorado Springs, CO: NavPress, 1994, 2002), 34.
4. Marita Bonner, as quoted in Sarah Ban Breathnach, *Simple Abundance* (New York, NY: Warner Books, 1995).
5. Henry Cloud and John Townsend, *Safe People* (Grand Rapids,

MI: Zondervan, 1995), 11.

6. Adapted from a presentation made at the Southern California Women's Retreat, Anaheim, CA, 2001.

7. Lewis, *The Four Loves,* 61.

Chapter 4

1. Mitch Albom, *Tuesdays With Morrie* (New York, NY: Broadway Books, 1997), 52.

2. Rebecca West, Irish critic, journalist, and novelist (1892–1983) (*www.quotationspage.com/quote/1747.html*).

3. *www.quoteland.com/author.asp?AUTHOR_ID=822*

4. As quoted in Ban Breathnach, *Simple Abundance,* November 2.

5. Ban Breathnach, *Simple Abundance,* November 18.

6. Dee Brestin, *The Friendships of Women,* (Colorado Springs, CO: Victor Books, 1988, 1995, 1997), 70.

7. Will Durant, quote from commencement address "We Have a Right to Be Happy Today" (*www.willdurant.com/youth.htm*).

8. John Eldredge, *The Journey of Desire* (Nashville, TN: Thomas Nelson, 2000), 96.

9. Donald Miller, *Blue Like Jazz* (Nashville, TN: Thomas Nelson, 2003), 232.

Chapter 5

1. *Serendipity Bible for Groups, 3rd edition* (Littleton, CO: Serendipity House, 1998), 1,795.

2. Marita Littauer. Used by permission. This is one of several ways to categorize the various personalities.

3. Corrie Cutrer, "Power of Two," *Today's Christian Woman* (July/August 2003): 36.

4. L.B. Cowman, *Streams in the Desert* (Grand Rapids, MI: Zondervan, 1996), 123.

5. Quoted in Hunter and Larson, *In the Company of Friends,* 70.

6. Dr. David White, pastor of NorthPark Community Church, Santa Clarita, California.

7. Brestin, *The Friendships of Women,* 91-92.

8. *www.trueinsights.com/quotes/2/2*

9. Hallmark, Fresh Ink (Hallmark Cards. Inc., Kansas City, MO 64141).

Chapter 6

1. As quoted in Dianna Booher, *Fresh-Cut Flowers for a Friend* (Dallas, TX: Word Publishing, 1997), 74.
2. *NIV Study Bible, 10th Anniversary Edition* (Grand Rapids, MI: Zondervan, 1995), 944.
3. Oswald Chambers, *My Utmost for His Highest* (Uhrichsville, OH: Barbour, 1963), March 23.
4. *www.quotesandpoem.com/quotes/listquotes/author/george_bernanos*
5. Rebecca Wells, *Divine Secrets of the Ya-Ya Sisterhood* (New York, NY: HarperCollins, 1996), 296.

Chapter 7

1. Booher, *Fresh-Cut Flowers for a Friend*, 53.
2. Lewis, *The Four Loves*, 62.
3. Brestin, "The Power of Two," *Today's Christian Woman*, 32.
4. John and Stasi Eldredge, *Captivating* (Nashville, TN: Thomas Nelson, 2005), 12.
5. Valerie Monroe, "Life Isn't a Beauty Contest," *O, Oprah's magazine* (August 2002): 165.
6. Brennan Manning, author, said this at a retreat at Christ Lutheran Church in Valencia, California, January 26, 2007.

Chapter 8

1. A.W. Tozer, *The Pursuit of God* (Camp Hill, PA: Christian Publications, Inc., 1982), 22.
2. Rick Warren, *The Purpose-Driven Life* (Grand Rapids, MI: Zondervan, 2002), 64.
3. Dee Brestin, *The Colors of His Love* (Nashville, TN: W Publishing Group, 2002), 115.
4. Hunter and Larson, *In the Company of Friends*, 142.

Chapter 9

1. *Webster's Ninth New Collegiate Dictionary*, (Springfield, MA: Merriam-Webster, Inc., 1983), 602.

Chapter 10

1. Brestin, *The Friendships of Women,* 128.
2. Adapted from an idea from Marty Russell at the NorthPark Community Church women's retreat.
3. Beth Moore, *Breaking Free* Workbook, Group Session #7 "The Potter and the Clay" (Nashville, TN: LifeWay Church Resources, 1999), 158.
4. Reference to Rebecca Wells, *Divine Secrets of the Ya-Ya Sisterhood* (New York, NY: HarperCollins, 1996).
5. L.B. Cowman, *Streams in the Desert* (Grand Rapids, MI: Zondervan, 1997), 315.
6. Quoted in Ban Breathnach, *Simple Abundance,* September 28.
7. Hunter and Larson, *In the Company of Friends,* 24.
8. *www.momsintouch.org*

Chapter 11

1. Tracy Klehn, *Prayer Starters for Busy Moms* (Bloomington, MN: Bethany House, 2006), 61.
2. Lewis, *The Four Loves,* 66.
3. Dr. Avedis Panajian.

Chapter 12

1. As quoted in Ban Breathnach, *Simple Abundance,* November 18.
2. As quoted in Hunter and Larson, *In the Company of Friends,* 33.
3. Robert Robinson, "Come, Thou Fount of Every Blessing" (Public Domain, 1758), *www.cyberhymnal.com.*
4. Helen Keller, *http://en.wikiquote.org/wiki/Helen_Keller.* Unsourced.